SOVEREIGNTY

The Tao Principle of Self Management

Samuel Beasley

ISBN-13: 978-1717419460
ISBN-10: 1717419461

DEDICATION

Dear Grandchildren, this book is dedicated to you and to your grandchildren.

CONTENTS

Section Two

A Study of Virtue

Section Three

Working on
The Self

ACKNOWLEDGMENTS

(A STUDY IN GRATITUDE)

This work and publication would not be possible without the spiritual and editing support of Carrie Ritts. Without her help and influence this effort would be no more than a conglomeration of obnoxious conjecture. Thank you, Carrie.

I cannot begin to convey the importance of Derek Lin's work and his devotion to Tao Studies. Without the clarity of accurate and thorough translations of ancient Chinese, into modern western vernacular, we would be subject to misdirection and an inaccurate understanding of the Tao Te Ching Classic. So much can be, and is often, lost with other translators, yet Derek is far and away the best at bridging the gap between ancient and modern Chinese and English. Perhaps the greatest gift of all is that of showing us how to implement these priceless lessons in everyday modern life. On behalf of all of us in the low places, thank you Derek.

To my Sifu Chun Zeng (aka Leianna Rackliff) who introduced me to Chinese culture and history. She has been my friend, my coach, and my resource for cultivating Nei Gong (internal arts). I have the honor of being one of her first American friends and sincerely hope that I have been a good one.

And to my family, who continues to treat me with tolerance, patience, and love. I am eternally grateful.

And to you, dear reader and fellow traveler along the way, thank you for having the curiosity and interest to purchase this book and give it consideration. I hope you find some small insight that benefits you in a meaningful and beneficial way.

INTRODUCTION

Why You Should Try This Book

What is your single biggest dream? What is it you are hoping for? This book you are holding is a handbook for staying on the path to achieve a successful and happy life. The way forward, to realize your hopes and fulfill your dreams, is broad and plain yet so many of us fail. Why do we stray from the path that takes us closer to those dreams? Why do we lose our way and repeatedly fail to realize those dreams? Only through the willpower and self-discipline as the Sovereign can you transform your life. Cultivating sovereignty is a life-long commitment of mindfully attending to your path. This book is a collection of some Tao strategies for developing sovereignty. These are some that enabled me to realize some effective powerful insights for success.

Failure has been defined as a lack of success. Success has been defined as the realization or accomplishment of an intended goal, achievement, or objective. Failure and success are part of life with the realization that either is determined by the choices and actions we take. Success happens when we can use discipline to make choices and take actions that keep us on the course to reach our objectives. Failure is making choices and taking actions that corrupt our efforts to stay on course. Self-Discipline is the determining factor for failure and success. This book shows you how discipline of the self will determine your destiny. Life with its successes and failures is a journey of self-discovery. If you approach your self-discovery honestly you will realize things about your 'self' that you have not realized before. These become the things that you work on.

This handbook is a guide based on the ancient wisdom of the Tao Te Ching. I discovered that the problems, suffering, and desires of people from ancient times were not too different from modern society. Only our means of coping and self-destruction are more sophisticated.

How to Use This Book

This is a handbook for the cultivation of discipline. You can read it in a linear fashion from front to back. However, it is designed to assist you in your journey of self-discovery, so you can start where you feel it is most relevant. What is the biggest hope or dream you wish to achieve? With that question in mind, browse the book looking for the areas of focus that speak to you. What would you like to change? Be honest about why you have failed before, and look for the guidance that will lead you to success.

"A journey of a thousand miles begins beneath the feet"
Chapter 64, Verses 9-10, Tao Te Ching

I know what it's like to hit the wall. Life can become such a mess that you feel too overwhelmed by defeat and failure to know where to begin. The journey begins in the simplest way possible. It is right here, right now, where you are. Your journey begins with the first step. Each step is a moment of truth in which the direction you step in either takes you closer to success or further away. Chapter 26 is titled, "Work On The Self, First." By working on the self you will cultivate the discipline to keep moving in the right direction. Use the way of virtue to consciously step in the right direction.

In self-reflection you can realize what you should have done and thus learn from your failure by taking the correct action steps next time around. The power of the Tao Te Ching is understanding which discipline/s to choose and implement for the situation you are in. Thus, through the universal law of cause and effect, or karma, you will unify with the creative force to realize true success.

Glossary and Index

Try the glossary and index in the back of the book to map your way. The insights and principles in this book are all connected in ways that complement each other. You will begin to discover things about yourself that you never realized before. You will be lead to different chapters and areas of focus.

Be Honest with Your Self

Take ownership of your own role in where you find yourself in life. It is important not to be under or over judgmental of the choices that got you here. Just be honest and accurate. Don't live under illusions that the ego will offer up to make you feel better. Instead just accept the truth of your part and move forward with the discipline to no longer repeat those choices and behaviors that continue to result in failure.

Take Notes – Keep a Journal

As you experience this journey of self-discovery, take notes. There are blank pages at the end of each chapter, so when you discover an insight you can write it down immediately. I recommend that you keep a journal of the insights about your self-discovery. In a sense you will be creating your own handbook for successful living. You will be invited to meditate, through self-reflection, about the what, why, and how that make you feel the way you do and make the choices you did to create the destiny you are experiencing.

Don't Give Up

"I never lose. Either I win or I learn." Nelson Mandela

Don't give up when you face an obstacle. Finish what you start. Learn from mistakes by working on your discipline. Next time you face a problem use it as an opportunity use willpower and discipline to move forward without repeating the same old mistakes. During the day make a note, and when you can search the teachings in this book to help you formulate your game plan.

Start Small and Evolve Naturally

One of the most powerful virtues is moderation. Through discipline of the self you can side step the ego's desire of instant gratification and be patient. Just work on your life one step at a time. Learn, grow, and experience life fully.

This is a lifelong process. Our cultivation of self-awareness and discipline never ends. Follow these teachings and you will experience true success without striving and with a seemingly effortless achievement.

Get A Copy of the Tao Te Ching

I use Derek Lin's, *Tao Te Ching- Annotated and Explained*. This book, along with weekly in-depth lessons, will focus a deep understanding of the principles and insights. Each week there is a live presentation on what each character, each word, and each chapter mean. More importantly they give invaluable insight into how they are applied in modern times.

.

You can view these lessons on **Youtube** at: Tao Talks with Derek Lin, https://www.youtube.com/c/taotalks.

 I invite you to visit the home page at: http://taoism.net

Facebook: https://www.facebook.com/groups/tao.talks/

Now, here is another moment of truth. Do you give these lessons a try or just stay on same path hoping for something to change? If you give this path a serious effort, I am confident that your life will significantly change for the better.

SECTION ONE – TAO PRINCIPLES

SECTION ONE – TAO PRINCIPLES

SECTION ONE
A Study of Tao Principles

To understand the Tao as a spiritual and philosophical way of life it helps to have a fundamental understanding of some of its basic principles. These principles make up its structure and describe to a tiny degree how the universe works. Even though humanity has made some wonderful discoveries, through physics, a complete understanding of the cosmos is still a long way out. The good news is that if you are able to implement just a quantum of Tao virtue you will transform your life.

The principles that I list here are strictly my observation and conjecture of a few of the basics. These are just glimpses of the Tao passed on to us from the ancients. They are observations by devotees of the Tao since before recorded history. Twenty-Five Hundred years ago the author of the Tao Te Ching introduced the Tao by informing us in the first two verses of Chapter One,

> *"The Tao that can be spoken is not the eternal Tao*
> *The name that can be named is not the eternal*
> *name"*

For the sake of conversation and discussion, it is called Tao.[1] You must be wary of the ego whose ignorance convinces itself that it knows something by naming it. This

---

1 See the chapter on_The Tao Te Ching

book about sovereignty is specific to controlling the ego
and therefore the ego-perspective. To understand the Tao
you must be empty of entrenched opinions and ignorance
and be open minded.

> "...In understanding in all directions
> Can one be without intellectuality...?"
> excerpt from Chapter 10, Tao Te Ching[2]

You will find that Tao principles have a complementary
relationship with one another. They also integrate with
virtue and become the foundation for the other sections of
the book (Virtues and Strategies). Becoming a Tao
cultivator is to practice living in accordance with the nature
of the universe. Aligning spirit/consciousness with this
greater cosmic nature is to attain the the Tao. The
discipline of following this path is sovereignty.

I have observed what seems to be a corresponding
similarity with Tao concepts and Quantum Theory.
Interestingly, others far more educated than I have made
similar observations. The similarity is resonant enough that
a strong sense of clarity can be found in practicing these
important Tao concepts.

I strongly advise that you pay attention to intention as you
seek to understand the Tao teachings. Be honest and be
aware when you find your ego seeking knowledge for the
reasons of cleverness. The pursuit of knowledge is just

---

2 Chapter 10 of the Tao Te Ching deals specifically with cultivating Mystic
Virtue. Intellectuality is an ego feature to be mindful of showing off.

another ego trap, and you can be distracted from the powerful insight that awaits you as a cultivator of sovereignty.

SECTION ONE – TAO PRINCIPLES

1

SOVEREIGNTY

In governing people and serving Heaven
There is nothing like conservation
Only with conservation is it called submitting early
Submitting early is called emphasis on accumulating virtues
Accumulating virtues means there is nothing one cannot overcome
When there is nothing that one cannot overcome
One's limits are unknown
The limitations being unknown, one can possess sovereignty
With this mother principle of power, one can be everlasting
This is called deep roots and firm foundation
The Tao of longevity and lasting vision
Chapter 59, Tao Te Ching

What Is Sovereignty

I define a Sovereign as one who is the supreme authority or ruler over a domain. You can think of it as being the leader of a country like a President, a Prime Minister, a King or a Queen. Sometimes these supreme rulers are great leaders and are loved by the people, and sometimes they are hated as wicked despots. History remembers them as benevolent and wise leaders. Modern society has memorialized their words as common sayings. And you can look back through history and see where the powerful tyrants have created catastrophe and suffering. These types of monarchs have left devastation and are remembered as examples of humanity's dark side.

For a moment think of yourself as a Czar and the empire you rule over is your life. Within this dominion are the people you interact with and the challenges experienced. As the ruler over your life, how is it going? As the president of your life your choices and decisions play a prominent role in both the present moment and your future. The seeds of the future, your destiny, are planted in the present moment. The present moment you are experiencing now began in your past. As the top decision maker, what kind of life have you created?

This book is about how you can become a successful and efficient ruler through consciously cultivating sovereignty. Sovereignty is more than just a term; it is a state of being. It is being self-aware and mindful of how you perceive reality along with wise choices and right actions. It is a management system implemented in a state of self-awareness. This self-awareness is an awakened state, as a spiritual being, managing and experiencing life.

Sovereignty is a perpetual state of self-discipline through self-awareness. Sovereignty is discipline over the ego sense of self or the ego identity. Sovereignty is actualized through

6

choices while being in the highest state of consciousness which is "self-awareness." Self-awareness is the realization that you are a spiritual being experiencing life in a physical plane.

This state of being transcends identity and is much more than just your thoughts and the mind. You are the consciousness that has the moment by moment experience as a physical being. This detached state of being is referred to as the silent witness or the observer. I have observed Taoist refer to this transcended self as "true self."

Why Sovereignty?

"...With this mother principle of power [sovereignty], one can be everlasting

This is called deep roots and firm foundation

The Tao of longevity and lasting vision..."

Verses 9-11

Some key words to note here are *"everlasting, longevity and lasting vision."* Sovereignty is the *mother principle of power* which gives you endurance to experience a long physical life and evolve spiritually (enlightenment). Sovereignty is the constancy of spirit. Sovereignty is being. Sovereignty is the Tao (the way) of longevity and lasting vision. Therefore, you should cultivate Sovereignty as if your life depended on it because guess what, it does. Sovereignty is being the ruler over the emotional, desire seeking ego so that you can attain the Tao.

Consider these words again:

"...Accumulating virtues means there is nothing one cannot overcome

When there is nothing that one cannot overcome

One's limits are unknown..."

Verses 5-7

Sovereignty

Sovereignty

2

THE TAO TE CHING

Master Po: "Your feet tread heavily on the ground, have you a burden grasshopper?"
Disciple Caine: It is my thoughts that carry the weight Master. I've been in the marketplace, where the men there argue and fight. There's no peace.
Master Po: "Why does that trouble you while your home is here?"
Disciple Caine: "I want all men to know peace."
Master Po: "It is written in the Tao Te Ching,
'under heaven, all can see beauty as beauty,
only because there is ugliness.
All can know good as good
only because there is evil.
Therefore, having and not-having risen together.
Difficult and easy complement each other.
High and low rest upon each other.
Front and back follow one another.
From the Television Show Kung Fu[3]

Choice is action and is the causation for your destiny. So, in each moment of choice from what sources should you turn to for guidance?

The television show *Kung Fu* was popular in the mid 70's. Viewers recognized the wisdom of the Tao and Chan

---

[3] KUNG FU, AND AMERICAN TV SERIES WHOSE SEASONS RAN ROM 1972 -1975. IT STARRED DAVID CARRADINE (AS KWAI CHANG CAINE) ET AL. MASTER PO IS PLAYED BY ACTOR KEYE LUKE. THE SERIES WAS PRODUCED BY WARNER BROTHERS FOR ABC.

Buddhist teachings while watching stories of Kwai Chang Caine's coming of age and exploration of America. The popularity of the show revealed that the lessons are as timeless and as relevant today as they were in 1972, as well as is the time of Lao Tzu. Kung Fu was a relatively unknown martial art and became a favorite aspect of the show. You may find it interesting to watch the show and look for the lessons of wisdom to be found in each episode.

About the Tao Te Ching

(Pronounced Dow-Duh-Jing).[4]

Briefly, the Tao Te Ching is a collection of ancient Tao classics written down by the Chinese sage, Lao Tzu. Contrary to popular belief, Lao Tzu did not invent Taoism. As you can see in the verse below, Lao Tzu refers to the ancients before his time as the "Tao of the ancients."

"Wield the Tao of the ancients." Chapter 14, Verse 18

The roots of Taoism are buried in the antiquity of at least 5000 years ago. Its shamanic origins have been traced back to tribal beliefs of a people living in an area of the Yellow River of Northern China. [5] Thousands of years later, Lao Tzu wrote the Tao Te Ching based on what his generation understood to be the true Tao. Therefore many people consider him the father of philosophical Taoism. There is some argument as to whether Lao Tzu was real, or just a mythological figure or the belief of a group of Tao scholars

---

[4] For an accurate translation and explanation of the Tao Te Ching, please visit www.taoism.net, I also recommend Derek Lin's Book, Tao Te Ching – Annotated & Explained

[5] Eva Wong; Taoism. Shambhala Publications

of the time. Regardless of the source of the Tao Te Ching, it is now regarded as a priceless source of Tao wisdom.

I have found the wisdom of the Tao to be a practical yet powerful philosophical guide to cultivating spirituality and a more successful life. Even though these concepts are ancient, they are as relevant now as they were back in antiquity. While we may live in the age of advanced technology and social democracy you can see that people at every level suffer and have misery. We often read about a celebrity who has both fame and fortune yet chooses to end his or her own life due to extreme unhappiness. Just like in ancient times, there are the working poor who suffer while catering to the pompous elite. Whether it was a peasant from long ago or the working poor in a modern-day sweatshop, people still suffer. Whether rich or poor, people seek harmony and an end to suffering. These philosophical and spiritual teachings offer a way to find harmony and the Tao of joy. You can learn how to make the best of situations and to at least stop mental suffering and self-destructive behaviors. You can cultivate Sovereignty so that you can achieve the self-discipline and willpower to avoid the traps of the ego.

The name Tao Te Ching means "The Way of Virtue Classic. It is comprised of two sections that have been combined into one volume. The first section includes Chapters 1 through 37 and is referred to as "Tao Ching" pronounced 'Dow Jing.' The second section, Chapters 38 through 81, is known as Te Ching and is pronounced "Duh Jing." The Tao Ching means "The Way Classic" and is devoted to a study of the Tao as "the way." It discusses the Tao as both a way of spiritual cultivation and living and the Tao as a mysterious source. The second section, the Te Ching means" Virtue Classic" and is devoted to the study of virtue in the Taoist sense. When they were joined sometime later, the totality became "The Way of Virtue Classic;" The Tao Te Ching.

In these teaching are some interesting and profound perspectives that can illuminate the deeper insights of our life experiences. So many powerful concepts are lost when popular culture reduces the lessons to cliché. Virtues such as patience and simplicity can be quickly overlooked because they appear to have no importance.

The ego which seeks instant gratification will not perceive the power of these virtues. To the ego-self, virtue is a waste of time or an obstacle to satisfy the insatiable desire and never-ending hunger.

The chapters of this book list just a just few of these much deeper concepts so that you might see the deeper underlying reality. These virtues are the 'how and why' this path can be so powerful. These Tao principles and insights can create a foundation for developing sound strategies for maintaining sovereignty. As a Sovereign, you cultivate the discipline for staying on your true path.

The Tao Te Ching

3

THE TAO

The Tao that can be spoken is not the eternal Tao
The name that can be named is not the eternal name
The nameless is the origin of Heaven and Earth
The named is the mother of myriad things
Thus, constantly without desire, one observes its essence
Constantly with desire, one observes its manifestations
These two emerge together but differ in name
The unity is said to be the mystery
Mystery of mysteries, the door to all wonders.
Chapter 1, Tao Te Ching

Tao cultivators keep things simple. Keeping to simplicity, I recommend you view the Tao in two fundamental ways:

1. *As the source and creative energy of the universe*

2. *As a spiritual path that follows the natural order of the universe*

While Quantum physicists have uncovered many clues as to the origin and workings of the universe, many scientists admit that there is still much clouded in mystery. Throughout history, humanity has studied nature and the cosmos and noticed patterns and their emergent properties. Humans have learned to harness small fragments of nature to our benefit, yet much of nature is still untamed. The nature of the Tao is that there is an emergent property of creative energy. This mysterious property is unknowable in totality yet is the spontaneous creative power that has propagated since the initial big bang. Life is the conscious experience of this creative process and the myriad of things that come and go within it.

Sovereignty is the self-cultivation of being the ruler over the emotional mind (ego) and living in harmony with both aspects of the Tao. As a philosophical and spiritual path, the Tao cultivator lives by the principles of virtue that create harmony between the spiritual identity (higher consciousness) and emotional mind (ego). Guiding your life choices in conformity with virtue and Tao principles is called "The Way." Heaven is representative of spiritual consciousness and earth representative of the physical experience.[6] There are two states of being. They are known as spiritual and physical. They are both parts of the human experience whose unity is the great mystery. Sovereignty is the ability of spiritual consciousness to implement the virtue of discipline.

---

[6] Heaven and Earth are referred to frequently in Tao Study. (Spiritual/Physical realms.

This section of the book shares Tao principles that have been observed since the ancient times in China. There are more than what I have listed here, but these are some that I believe to be important for cultivating Sovereignty.

I have found that these principles overlap in both the spiritual and physical domains. By living in unity with the way of virtue you can better live in harmony with the Tao. To go against the essence of reality causes resistance and problems that are the root of self-destruction. However, this is the nature of the ego-mind; to self-destruct in the blind pursuit of satisfying the desire or reacting to an emotional state of mind. Sovereignty is the ability to transcend this ego path of striving and return to your essential nature. What is our true nature? To realize that we are a spiritual being in unity with nature. The quickest and easiest way to see the Tao in its purest form is to observe nature. The Tao is the way of living in harmony with the nature.

Following the Tao is hard when the ego is in charge. If the life of ego is all you know it becomes too easy to lose your way, make unnecessary mistakes, and experience self-destruction. It does not have to be that way. Here is a bit of advice from Lao Tzu that gives us the courage to stick to the path.

> *"...have a little knowledge*
>
> *Walking the great Tao*
>
> *I fear only to deviate from it*
>
> *The Tao is broad and wide*
>
> *But people take the side paths..."*
>
> *Chapter 53, Verses 1-5, Tao Te Ching*

Taking the side path is a distraction of the ego. Become the Sovereign and follow the great Tao which broad and wide.

The Tao

Meditation & Mindfulness

4

MEDITATION & MINDFULNESS

"...In holding the soul and embracing oneness
Can one be steadfast without straying...?"
Chapter 10, Verses 1 & 2, Tao Te Ching

Meditation and Mindfulness are the foundations of the spiritual path of the Tao cultivator. Their relevance becomes apparent when taking a close look at self-discipline. Self-discipline and self-control determine the choices that are made in the moment to moment experiences of life. The ability to make choices that keep the Tao cultivator on the path is super important. Being distracted is a loss of awareness. The loss of presence allows the ego-self to take over. The ego is a self-absorbed state of being that is driven by desire. It (ego) is constantly self-absorbed and experiencing anxiety at not having its desires fulfilled or resenting the reality it is experiencing. The ego experience is filled with stress and dark moods that lead to desperate self-

23

destructive choices. Desire, reaction, and coping make up the downward cycle. These are constants in the life of the ego, and they always lead to more suffering.

The meditative state is one of unity between spirit and mind. Clarity and calm abiding are the foundations for sovereignty (self-discipline). With the ego under firm management you can follow the ways of virtue and wisdom. The wisdom of the Sovereign realizes the result of cause and effect (karma). The way of virtue and wisdom produce harmony and longevity. The karma of ego choices leads to suffering and death.

Meditation

The essence of meditation is the awakening of aware-consciousness in the stillness between thoughts.

This awakening is a transcendental practice that focuses awareness and attention. Practice begins by concentrating the attention or mental focus through observation of a single focal point. It may sound easy in theory, but for beginners this can be difficult. Most people new to meditation are beset with wandering minds. Their attention jumps around from thought to thought. When the mind has been highly stimulated the inner focus will be chaotic. Many will quickly become lost and distracted in the messy mindstream of thinking. Meditation training is to continuously wake up from this chaos and bring awareness back into focus. A skillful meditation instructor will help by gently intervening to bring the wandering mind back to presence. With repetition, the student will start to become conditioned to return to presence on their own. You must practice over and over enough so that the brain and the mind will become conditioned to being present and paying attention. Being awake and mindful is known as self-awareness. It is the highest state of living consciousness. This higher state of consciousness is above the ego and known as the true self or spirit. This is the state of being of sovereignty. In this state you will no longer be attached or imprisoned by the ego and its distractions. It is a detached state of being that has a subjective relationship with thinking.

With practice, you can gain skill in discerning mental and emotional activities without being under their control. With the skill of waking up you will be able to pay attention to what is on your mind and do something about it.

Mindfulness

> *"Mindfulness means paying attention in a particular way; on purpose, in the present moment and non-judgmentally." Jon Kabat-Zinn*

When you have transcended the thinking mind, you

can observe and practice discernment[7] from a perspective of non-judgment. This intentional state of paying attention is called mindfulness. Free of the influence of emotional states of mind and ego you will be in a state of detachment (unattached action). Through self-reflection, you can realize the true nature of your mental state. Then, how you perceive reality is made through discernment and choice.

Why is this so important? Mindfulness and meditation are necessary to take charge of your destiny. Destiny is the result of choices you make each moment of each day. Sovereignty is the ability to take charge of your destiny and rule over the ego along with its influences over the mind and emotions. Therefore, to transform your life into one of joy and success you must cultivate the ability to practice mindfulness and be the Sovereign.

In cultivating the Tao of successful living ask yourself the question that Lao Tzu proposes in this line from Chapter 10,

> *"...In holding the soul and embracing oneness, can you be steadfast without straying...?"*

---

[7] Observing is to take notice or perceive. In this context, discernment is the term used for determining the nature of something without the judgement of it being good or bad. The lesson is to pay attention and discern meaning without the distraction of the value judgment (filter of 'good' or 'bad').

Stillness

Stillness is a state of being. It is found in the emptiness or void between the movements of the mind (thinking). Concentration and focus are skills cultivated through practice. Stillness is the domain of the silent observer or silent witness. This observer is the true self or spiritual identity. It is the highest form of consciousness. When you enter stillness you no longer identify as the ego (me), you become the no-self which is pure spirit. It is both nothing and everything.

Stillness is a "non-local" vantage point for observing and discerning reality. You may have heard the phrase "enter into stillness," which is transcendence. Stillness is a realized state of being that transcends the ego-state of mind and the chaos of incessant thinking. Within stillness, you will be able to detach from the distraction of the mindstream of thought.

Stillness is the highest level of being present. Also, and very importantly, you will be apart from the ego. Stillness and detachment are the gateways to unity with the Tao. It is the highest form of meditation. Stillness and detachment are a state of being. Similar practices are known as Samadhi or Satori. Unity with the Tao or attainment of the Tao is enlightenment.

Self-reflection

Self-Reflection meditation is a concentrated observation, or a meditation that reflects on your life and being able to view it through multiple perspectives. This is a kind of openness or emptiness that can free a person from the prison of mental activity. Reflecting on your experiences without self-praise or self-judgment is done through discernment of detached observation. There can be a sub-conscious influence on your outlook created by the ego. Empty of value-judgment you can see the reality of how things are rather than the illusions of the ego. In cultivating sovereignty, you will work towards understanding and implement the concept of emptiness as a source.

Contemplative meditation

Contemplative meditation is the ability to engage your mental properties, especially memory, and explore what you find with the ability to remain detached. The ability to concentrate the mind is an important skill that comes only through lots of practice. Being able to concentrate and direct mental focus to your spiritual will is the work of a Sovereign. Otherwise, without the skill of concentration, the distraction will set in, and the ego will resume control, and your mind will wander where desire takes it.

Exercise

Contemplate the insight of how emptiness can give function to a substance (form) for both the internal and the external.[8] This exercise is a meditation in its self. Being the Sovereign of your mental kingdom (your mind), it becomes

---

[8] See Chapter 10; Emptiness

possible to make better choices that create your quality of life. In stillness, the Sovereign can be open and able to provide the space for hope, possibility, inspiration, intuition, and change.

Hopefully, by now, you realize the necessity of meditation as the awakening process from the ego mind into pure being and spiritual awareness.

The Tao cultivator cannot begin working on self-control until he or she has developed enough skill to return often to the meditative state. Learning to meditate is a discipline and devotion. It is difficult because of a lack of self-discipline. The spirit (true self) must use discipline over the ego-self. Like anything else the more you practice, the better you get. Being Sovereign is to empty the heart and mind of ego hunger so that you create the space for awareness.

Detached from ego; the silent observer moves with the flow of the Tao without attachment to outcome or agenda. Hence, to practice the Tao and cultivate sovereignty, you must become skilled in meditation and mindfulness. In everyday life practice the ability to stay present and aware. Practice being mindful of what you are doing and why you are doing it. Then choose your next step wisely. Having the wisdom and knowing what virtue and action are best is what the Tao Te Ching teaches. Cultivate your Tao wisdom by seeking the insights of how the Tao works. Make choices of virtue rather than ego, and then implement a strategy for staying committed to your spiritual path.

Treat the practice of meditation as a personal discipline. Make your practice a routine whether you think you need it or not. Treat it as a high priority to supersede other activities. The brain has much plasticity. By repeating the practice over and over you will create a neural network[9] for returning to the awakened and relaxed state. It will get easier as time goes on. With diligence, presence will become effortless. This relaxed alert state of presence will carry over into your life as mindfulness.

Sovereignty is the state of consciously ruling your life from the foundation of spirit and virtue. Be the Sovereign.

---

[9] Neural network here means to form a habit, or to become second nature of being present. Mindfulness becomes your default conscious state.

5

KARMA

People do not fear death
How can they be threatened with death?
If people are made to constantly fear death
Then those who act unlawfully
I can capture and kill them
Who would dare?
There exists a master executioner that kills
If we substitute for the master executioner to kill
It is like substituting for the great carpenter to cut
Those who substitute for the great carpenter to cut
It is rare that they do not hurt their own hands
Chapter 74, Tao Te Ching

"The Great Executioner"

In any given moment, we plant the seeds of our destiny. Inner intentions drive the choices we make, so it is important to be aware of these moments. By reflecting on your past you can gain insight into how you arrived in your current situation.

32

The simplest perspective of Karma is to view it as a law of cause and effect. The two most important perspectives of cause and effect are the spiritual view and the physics theory. In Taoism and Buddhism it is a spiritual principle. In Taoism, it is both spiritual and philosophical.

The philosophy of Karma has the same principle found in physics. Results are always preceded by an action that produced it. In Taoism, both play a significant role in understanding how the Tao is reflected in the spiritual and physical realm. An even simpler way to put it is, "what comes around goes around." Alternatively, you may have heard "what you put out into the world comes back to you stronger or bigger."

Choice and Destiny

"If you want to know your past,

look at your present conditions.

If you want to know your future,

look at your actions today."

Chinese Proverb- Unknown

Choosing is an action, and the result or effect is destiny. In any given moment you plant the seeds of your future. Inner intentions drive the choices you make, so it is important to be aware of these moments. By reflecting on your past, you can gain insight into the circumstances you realize in the present. These conditions, whether right or bad, are the result of earlier choices. Or they may be the result of someone else's choice. So, you can see how important the action of choosing is. Not only is it guaranteed to affect your future, but it may, and often does, influence the future of others.

It is essential that you understand the following points:

- Karma does not play favorites.

- No one can escape Karmas influence or the destiny they create.

- Seeds are planted to grow a garden. What you plant now is what you will reap later (the garden is a metaphor for your life).

- Choices create destiny. What you choose now creates the circumstances of your future (or the future of someone else). The results may come sooner or later.

A crucial insight is to realize and accept your responsibility for the circumstances of your life right now. In some ways, it does not matter if the current situation is a result of your choice or caused by something or someone else. Right here, right now, you are experiencing the results.

Things happen to us, expected and unexpected, self-caused, or not. Be aware of how you react to the things you experience whether you caused them or not. When something happens, it is typical to react. This reaction becomes a choice with a future result. So even if you did not cause this problem, be mindful of how your response will create even more karma results. If you did make a bad choice, be careful to understand what went wrong so you don't repeat the results.

How to Live with Karma

Instead of automatically reacting when something happens, you can, in a moment of self-awareness, consider what the wise choice should be. Being able to stop and think about the smart choice requires a degree of mindfulness. Mindfulness is something you cultivate as an extension of meditation.[10]

Now that you are present and mindful of choice, how do you know what to choose? That is where the wisdom of the Tao Te Ching (the way of virtue) can play a decisive role. Free of automatically reacting, you can let the wise insights and strategies of the Tao Te Ching guide you. Good intentions are not enough.

You must consult experience and wisdom to know what the right action is. It can be the wisdom of the Tao, and it can be your wisdom cultivated over a lifetime of experience. You may have heard the saying "the road to hell is paved with good intentions." Be patient and make a wise choice for the action that seems best.

---

[10] See Chapter 5, Meditation & Mindfulness

Consider this four-step process:

1. Be mindful of reaction.

- Be patient and don't automatically react.
- Stop and look at what is going on in your mind.
- Ask if an immediate response is even necessary.

2. What is your immediate reaction?

- What is the deeper intention?
- Are you blaming someone or something else?
- Can you take ownership of the bad choices you made in the past?
- What are you doing, and why are you doing it?
- What will the outcome be?
- What seeds am I planting?
- Is the ego at work?
- Is this virtuous?
- What might be the cause and effect of my actions?

3. Let wisdom guide you.

- What outcome would be best for everyone?
- What are some virtuous choices?
- What would your spiritual teacher or role model tell you to do?

4. Consider the wisdom of the Tao. What are some relevant Tao strategies?

- Consider the wisdom from what you have learned from your experiences.

HOW SOVEREIGNTY HELPS WITH KARMA

Cultivating Sovereignty is learning to rule your inner kingdom so that when you experience problems or obstacles, you will act wisely. The wise ruler can be aware of the inevitable changes that each day brings. Rather than resist the reality of impermanence, the sovereign cultivator integrates with the corresponding relationship of change, creation, and karma. Sovereignty will allow you to unify with the Tao and navigate your life through wise choices. Remember the four-step process. In this way, you create your true destiny.

In ancient times Karma was referred to as "The Great Executioner." It is a good idea to have a healthy respect for karma. Inevitably you will reap what you sow. Are you familiar with the saying "what goes around comes around?"

What you send out, the actions you take, will work its way back around gaining strength. When it fulfills its cycle and arrives back, it will be bigger. So, it is with great care that you create the moments of your life. This Tao principle is unavoidable, inescapable, and guaranteed. This convergence of karma with the present moment can be catastrophic; hence the saying *"the great executioner."* Like nature, the Tao does not play favorites. No one escapes the effect of karma. When and where the convergence happens is unknown and unpredictable. It may return very soon, or it may not catch up to you until another life time. You can run, but you cannot hide.

6

MYSTIC VIRTUE

"...Mystic Virtue is so profound, so far-reaching
It goes opposite to material things
Then it reaches great congruence..."
Chapter 65, verses 13-15, Tao Te Ching

What is mystic virtue and why is it so important? Its power is realized when the other virtues reach congruence.[11] Masters and Sages who have integrated this aspect of sovereignty are sought out because of their great wisdom and success at life. Their powers are mysterious and profound. They accomplish great things effortlessly and with joy. Because of this mysterious ability, people seek their guidance. They are loved and cherished.

There are two important aspects of mystic virtue to study: the "Inherent Power" of virtue, and the right choice of "The Two Standards."

Inherent Power

A study of mystic virtue is one of cultivating a mysterious and unusual power. However, this power is not what you might think. Tao masters and sages attain different kinds of power. Think of someone in your society who you think of as powerful. Consider what kind of power or powers they

---

[11] Congruence is defined as an agreement, coming together into harmony. See Chapter 25 "Harmony".

wield. Examples might be the Mayor of your city or town, your Commanding Officer, your professor, or your boss. Maybe you are thinking about a mighty bull or some powerful beast. Perhaps you are even considering a shaman who can conjure the wind and rain.

While these are all examples of power, the power I am talking about is altogether different. It is something called inherent power.

An observation of inherent power reveals that it is hiding in plain sight. You may have used it or have been witness to it at various times but maybe never viewed it as significant. What I speak of is the power of virtue. Virtue has two meanings. The obvious one is the one we know as being of high moral standard or action. The other one is as an inherent power.

Consider these examples:

- *"by virtue of* her patience and self-discipline, she was able to lose 100 pounds."
- *"by virtue of* his reputation of honesty, he was able to gain the trust of the staff."

Change the phrase "by virtue of" to "because of" and you will gain the insight of inherent power. Masters and sages incorporate this power so skillfully that they make the hardest tasks or goals seem easy. They can share insights that bring clarity to murkiness. There is a definite level of mystique in how they always seem to know and see clearly, and so it gained the description of "mystic "(mysterious). Thus, it became known as "mystic virtue."

The Two Standards

The essence of mystic virtue is to be mindful of the two standards (virtue vs ego) and to take the right action. The simplest way to think about it is the right way and the wrong way, or wise way and ignorant way. You will activate inherent power when you are aware of ego intentions but hold to the way of virtue. In every moment you have a choice between spirit and ego objectives. To know both standards but to hold to virtue is called mystic virtue. Three chapters in the Tao Te Ching show us how to cultivate and attain this mysterious power; chapters 10, 51, and 65.

In each of these chapters there are what Lao Tzu refers to as the two standards. The Tao cultivator is to recognize the two standards and take the right action (choice). The two standards are: those based on ego and those that follow virtue. As you go through each of these chapters, look for the two standards and understand how Lao Tzu is encouraging you to choose the way of mystic virtue.

Chapter 10 - addresses the mindset for cultivating and exercising mystic virtue. The two standards are self-awareness vs. distraction (true self vs. ego). You cannot choose the right action (virtue) without being self-aware and mindful of ego influences.

<u>Chapter 51</u> - describes how the Tao produces, raises, shapes, and perfects balance in the universe. It does this spontaneously through its constant nature. Its inherent virtues and right actions are,

---

"...Produces without possession.

Acts without flaunting

Nurtures without domination..."

The Tao naturally produces (creates) without possessing. Living creatures are free to take from nature all of what they need. Nature, having no ego, acts without showing off. It nurtures (sustains us) without any need to control or dominate.

<u>Chapter 65 -</u> instructs us on using mystic virtue in interpersonal relationships and governing our lives (sovereignty).

Here is a consolidated list of virtuous standards compiled from the three chapters:

- Be steadfast without straying (self-aware/mindful).
- Be without imperfections (seeing reality as it is).
- Concentrate the energy and reach relaxation like an infant (relaxed and free of stress).
- Be without manipulation in your interactions (the feminine principle).[12]
- Create without possession (free of attachment to outcome and personal gain).
- Achieve without arrogance (humility).
- Raise without domination (help or assist without expectation or compensation).
- Produces but does not possess (gives freely)
- Act but not flaunt (action without ego vanity).
- Nurture but not dominate (holding to the feminine principles).
- Simplicity rather than cleverness in dealing with people (honesty, simple)
- Know the ego way but choose the Tao (the way of virtue, right action).

Look for the inherent power in choosing the right standard. In the list above, put the phrase "by virtue of being ..." in front of each line. Consider what the mystic power will produce.

Example: By virtue of being steadfast without straying I was able to (fill in the blank).

If you are a leader, think of your subjects. If you are a

---

[12] The feminine principle is yin in nature. Yielding, tranquil, nurturing (without domination), and most importantly, the giver of life.

parent, think of your children. Can you raise without domination? If you are a boss, think of your employees. Can you nurture without domination? Be the Sovereign in both the inner and outer world. Be mindful of the Two Standards and choose the action that is the way of mystic virtue. If you do this with consistency, you will cultivate inherent power. Cultivating Mystic Virtue is the way of the Sovereign, at one with the Tao.

A Matter of Perspective

A Matter of Perspective

7

A MATTER OF PERSPECTIVE

The sages have no constant mind
They take the mind of the people as their mind
Those who are good, I am good to them
Those who are not good, I am also good to them
Thus the virtue of goodness
Those who believe, I also believe them
Those who do not believe, I also believe them
Thus the virtue of belief
The sages live in the world
They cautiously merge their mind for the world
The people all pay attention with their ears and eyes
The sages care for them as children
Chapter 49, Tao Te Ching

A friend of mine told a story about his neighbor that I would like to share. The neighbor was a man who had a pet peeve about dog owners who would not pick up their pooch's poop while out for a walk. He was particularly perturbed if the poop was left in his front yard. One morning he saw a big pile of fresh poop steaming on his front lawn, and he became incensed. Irritated, he picked up the mess and once again his front yard was clean and flawless. The next morning, he found another fresh pile in his front yard. He was infuriated enough that he paid a visit to his neighborhood association to complain about it and to see if they had seen the dog that did it. Since no one had seen it happen, everyone agreed that it must have happened before daylight. So, the man got up early and tried to keep watch to catch the culprit. Try as he might he could never catch it. It was a mystery. Somehow it just appeared. After a week of this insulting dilemma he went to the homeowner's association to complain. When they told him that there was nothing they could do, he threatened legal action.

Frustrated, he bought an expensive security camera with night vision and motion sensors which enabled him to automatically video anyone who came along the sidewalk or into his front yard. Eagerly he set up the camera and retired to his bed.

The next morning there was a fresh pile in the same spot as all the others had been. Excitedly he went to his computer to view the recorded video. He watched the nights activities until finally toward the end of the clip; he saw something. The man's jaw dropped as he watched the video. He stood there stunned.

What he saw was his dog enter the screen from the side, walk over to the spot and drop a load of poo right where all the others had been. The man went out into the backyard and glared at his dog wondering how it had happened. With some investigation, he found the place that his dog had been escaping. All along it was his dog doing the dirty deed. This true story can show how quickly a change in perspective can reveal an underlying truth. The ego can play tricks with our reality.

PERSPECTIVE AS A MATTER OF CHOICE

Without clarity[13] truth can be deceptive and elusive. However, when you have clarity and can utilize the ability to see things from a different perspective you gain important insight. Define clarity as seeing things as they are and not the way of ego illusion. An illusion is something wrongfully perceived that gives a deceptive impression. When the mind is under the influence of ego, the intention and emotions of the moment will frame perspective. This perspective is all that the ego can reach.

The alternative is to detach and rise above this state of mind. Mindfulness is the ability to pay attention in a non-judgmental way and observe the different perspectives. With this clarity you will be able to see things as they are and make wiser choices. You will still make mistakes, however; by gaining clarity you will get closer to the mark.

---

[13] See the Chapter on Constancy and Spiritual Clarity.

People perceive the same thing in different ways. For instance, look at the figure. What do you see?

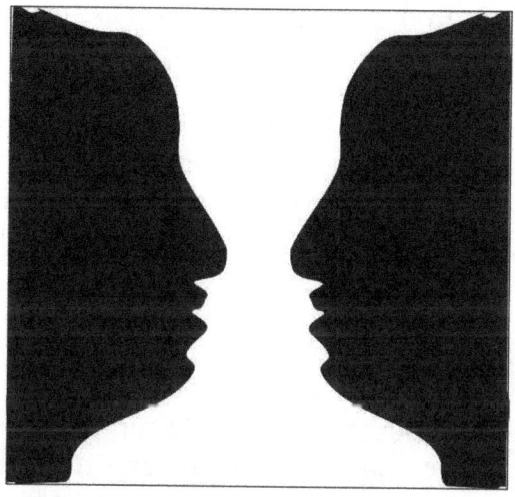

Clarity is the foundation for sovereignty. Seeking truth is something we do many times a day. Our beliefs are something we choose and can change. Truth is often a subjective matter of perspective. Perspective is elastic and constantly changing. Often, the illusion of truth tricks us. Two people will often view the same circumstance with different perspectives because of their different experiences in life. From these different experiences and perspectives arise different truths. Since truth is subjective and not absolute you can realize that your truth may not be the same as someone else's. Seeing the perspective from someone else's point of view is the beginning of empathy. Empathy leads to compassion.

What do you see in the drawing above? Do you see two people talking or a vase?

Hopefully, you can see both. Notice how the mind can switch perspective and meaning back and forth. This simple optical illusion shows how perception is subjective. If you are seeking the truth, how will you know which is more truthful?

Sometimes life experiences are complex, and sometimes they are straightforward. The ego, which is a part of the physical mind-perspective is often dominant. So, emotion and desire influence perspective. The spiritual mind, the true self, can realize many perspectives and arrive at a more informed decision. Because it is aware of the ego perspective yet not captivated by it, it can look beyond and become aware of the many faces of subjectivity.

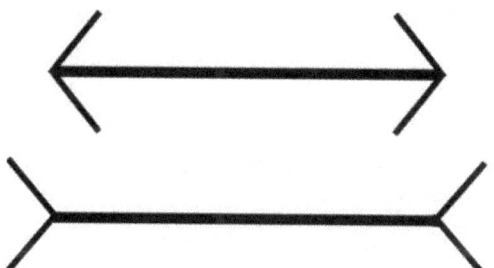

The center lines are identical but the optical illusion can make these seem to have different lengths

14

In the diagram above the two lines *seem* to be of different lengths, yet with a slight change in perspective you can realize that the arrowheads create an illusion. The mindful Sovereign realizes that perception can be filtered, tainted, and influenced by an overriding perspective. Sometimes things may seem to be one way only to conclude something else when examined closely. To be able to make wise, informed decisions you should consider what you perceive from different points of view.

---

[14] While I created the arrow sets above, the theory is credited to Franz Carl Muller-Lyer

Consideration is lost if you are mindlessly reactive. So, mindfulness of reaction is a good starting point. Being able to pay attention to the mind as it attaches itself to the first emotional reaction is an important skill to cultivate. Mindfulness is necessary for cultivating sovereignty. You remember the old saying about jumping to conclusions.

When you perceive that something is occurring in your life many points of view are available. When you are not mindful of your reactions you quickly and automatically default to the ego point of view. The Sovereign cultivator is grounded in the spiritual point of view and will seek multiple viewpoints for a deeper understanding. Negativity or desire will guide the ego-mind. Once you have considered the different points of view you can work on making a good choice. As mentioned in the last chapter there are two standards; to be mindful of the standard of ego and the standard of virtue. Ego reacts, and spirit follows the way of right action (wisdom).

Here are some examples of how the two standards give you a choice, depending on the condition of your mind and mood.

Ego	Vs.	Sovereignty
Reaction		Patience
Arrogance		Humility
Hatred		Love
Resentment		Acceptance
Judgment		Empathy
Fear		Courage
Desire		Satisfaction
Despair		Hope
Problems		Opportunities

Exercise. Try this two-step process to practice cultivate the ability to gain different perspectives. Think of something stressful that happened to you. It can be a personal interaction or an event that seemed to be a problem or obstacle.

Step 1. Pay attention and be mindful of ego reaction and step back into your higher awareness.

Step 2. Choose *to be patient* and delay reaction so that you can take a deeper look.

Step 3. Now put the situation in the center and walk around it (figuratively). Look at it from many points of view.

- What was your first reaction?

- What was your first initial point of view? Now set that aside and:

- Look at it from the other person's point of view.

- How would it look from the future (how important will this be a year from now)?

- How would it look from the past?

- How would you look at the situation if you loved them?

- How would you see the situation if you were related to the person involved?

- How would it look if you were friends?

- How would it look if you knew you could not fail?

- It is easy to see problems, but can you see opportunity?

- Do you even have to do something right now, or can you observe and see what happens next (can you be patient)?

Cultivating the self-discipline of sovereignty is following the way of virtue. The wisdom and power of the Tao are utilized when you consciously let virtue guide you in gaining clarity.

The following list are some of the virtues mentioned in the Tao Te Ching.

Think of that same interaction or event. How does it look from the perspective of:

- Compassion

- Conservation

- Humility

- Empathy

- Patience

- Wisdom

- Simplicity

- Moderation

- Softness

- Flexibility

- Harmony.

As you become skilled at being present, you will have the opportunity to practice gaining a better perspective in your daily life. Being present, your intuition can guide you. The more you practice the better you will become at discerning the truth in any given situation. The right perspective leads to right thinking which gives wisdom and power to the Sovereign.

A Matter of Perspective

8

YIELDING & FLEXIBILITY

"...Yield and remain whole
Bend and remain straight..."
Chapter 22, Verse 1 – 2, Tao Te Ching

Wisdom requires that you must be able to change perspectives when circumstances change. You must be flexible and willing to yield. There is a belief among Sovereign cultivators that it is important to be moderate and avoid absoluteness and rigidity of perspective.

One of the pitfalls of absolutism is that it is inflexible. When something is inflexible, it becomes too rigid and cannot change with its environment. For example, if a tree is flexible and it can bend with the force of each wind gust it tends to survive longer. Trees that are too rigid or too brittle will break when moved by the changing direction of the wind.

Being open-minded allows the assimilation of new data. An absolute perspective is inflexible and stunts growth and innovation. In your personal life, an absolute view will become your prison. So, for the sake of pragmatism, open your mind to the possibilities that are waiting for your discovery.

Wisdom is found in the understanding that most things you perceive in life are changing and impermanent.

Resistance to change is a common cause of anxiety and suffering. There are many reasons why you will not want change, but change is inevitable. Look for opportunities within change and it will help reduce stress. It is wise to accept and see things as they are. When you resist change on will only continue down the wrong path and lose sight of the right path. The right path is through virtuous choices.

So here is the BIG question. *How are you seeing life at this moment*? Waking up and paying attention to how you are seeing life in the 'right now' is an important step in gaining sovereignty over the emotional mind and the ego.

- Become aware of your current perspective and how what you are feeling is how you are seeing life right now. At this moment, be mindful and understand. Seek a way to choose a new perspective

- Notice the factors that influence the way you feel.

- Notice how the ego may be affecting decisions and choices.

- Notice how deep these feeling go.

- Ask yourself: How do I feel about the current situation?

In this moment lies the opportunity to raise your spirit. This is a powerful tool when you can make it work for.

Choice and destiny are complements of each other. Being able to raise your spirit becomes possible when you change your perspective.[15] For example, switch to the perspective of gratitude rather than resentment. Being able to be mindful of how you are seeing life at this moment is a very

---

[15] See Chapter 41, "Raising The Spirit".

powerful skill. It is the doorway to the mental prison that we lock ourselves in. Gaining a new perspective is the way to raise your spirit. It takes much practice. Moreover, that's what cultivation is. Cultivating these virtues in real life moments will help you to become skilled in paying attention to your reaction to life and the perspective that sets in. If you can be aware of it, then you can change it.

To be the effective ruler of your life, you must be effective in discerning the underlying reality. This wisdom is gained by intentionally knowing the many perspectives that abound. For every person, there is a unique perspective and a personal truth. You can get insight into these unique perspectives to help you solve problems and move beyond the inevitable conflicts.

 Seeing things from the perspective of another person can greatly assist in good interpersonal relationships. Think about it, the best friends are the ones who don't judge you and who like you as you are.

A change in perspective will help you see the opportunities that, at first glance, seemed to be problems. Seeing the many perspectives is how the Sovereign navigates through life- one step at a time. Seek the underlying reality by developing a multi-view perspective. Clarity through perspective cultivates sovereignty. Be the Sovereign.

Ying Yang

9

THE YIN – YANG PRINCIPLE

"Tao produces one
One produces two
Two produces Three
Three produce myriad things
Myriad things backed by yin and embracing yang
Achieve harmony by integrating their energy"
Excerpt from Chapter 42, Tao Te Ching

Wuji and Taiji

Wuji. "Tao produces one."

(symbol of Wuji)[16]

Before Yin – Yang there was/is Wuji. Wuji is the state of undifferentiated void that is full of potential and possibility.

---

[16] The Wuji symbol is denoted by an empty circle. This same circle becomes the Taiji Symbol when movement produces the yin/yang which are the white and black swirls)

64

In ancient philosophy it is the state before creation.[17] This emptiness is the nonpolarized state ripe with possibility. Some physicists theorize that before the creation of the universe, which is rapidly expanding, there was a state of high density and high temperature. Wuji would be the state before and the build-up for the potential creation of the universe. The high density/high-temperature state erupted in what is now called the "big bang." It is at this point that cosmological time began. Wuji is an emptiness of non-movement, non-action, and a state of unity. From the spiritual/philosophical perspective, Wuji is the stillness of the Tao full of potential, only needing consciousness to initiate creative intention.

Taiji. **"One produces two."**

The symbol for Taiji

Taiji is the state of movement that expands towards maximum polarity. From the nonpolarized and minimum state of Wuji, all elements of existence begin to separate and move towards the extreme. These two states of polarity are yin and yang.

---

[17] "For a biblical reference see Genesis1.1 & 1.2 from (New King James Version)

YIN & YANG - "THREE PRODUCES THE MYRIAD THINGS"

Before the big bang, the cosmos is theorized to have been in a state of collapse, or an extreme state of Yin (minimum movement yet full of potential). As potential built up in the form of density & temperature it reached the point of convergence it resulted in the big bang. This movement is the nature of the Tao with its creative force. With the big bang, the cosmos began a rapid expansion which is the nature of yang. Interestingly, the expansion is still increasing.

Understanding Yin & Yang is important because it is an aspect of the Tao that affects reality. All things, whether physical or ethereal, follow this principle. When you can unify your perspective of life with this principle things will begin to make sense and even have some understanding and predictability. Yin-Yang permeates everything that humans can conceive. It is especially helpful when contemplating energy or Qi. [18]This principle is the heart and soul of Taiji/Qigong.

Both domains, spiritual and physical (aka heaven and earth), interact and are interdependent upon each other. They permeate both the tangible and intangible always achieving balance. When balance is achieved, we will experience harmony. When balance is interrupted, discord arises and is experienced as destruction and suffering. Moving towards balance is the essential nature of the ever-changing, ever-flowing yin-yang principle of the Tao. In the

---

[18] Look up "potential difference or potential energy in your preferred reference source.

physical realm, stormy weather can be a clear example of vast energy moving, flowing and cycling through vast changes, with force as it seeks balance. The polarities of low and high pressure, dry and wet, warm and cold all interact in this balancing flow.

Stormy weather can also be a metaphor for the intangible when it describes relationships that are out of balance or not moving with the intention of balance. Both are apparent as moving energy. The elements in weather and emotional energy (feelings) follow the same principle. You can experience stormy weather both outside the body and inside the mind.

Patterns in Nature

Nature is a manifestation of the innate creative principle of the Tao. It is the myriad of things produced by the movement of the Yin and Yang. Insights about nature are insights into the workings of the Tao. You can see it in both living organisms and in the non-living aspects of the cosmos that we live in. The essential nature of yin and yang is change.

In the physical world, the weather is a good example for seeing how energy affects our weather and climate. The sun heats the water, air, and land. The build-up of temperature and density causes a change in the polarity of key sub-atomic particles. When this potential reaches a critical point, there will be a convergent release or *movement*. This is the same movement that you experience and realize this with the advent of lightning.[19]

YIN – YANG

Before separation and polarity there is stillness and calm. This is a state of Yin (diminished). Then the yang phase, or building begins. Energy particles begin to condense and to build potential. When it reaches fullness and reverses course back into a diminishing phase which is Yin. This movement towards balance is observed in the changing seasons and weather. It is one of the mysteries of the Tao.

The trend of the weather cycle can be seen from the greater perspective of climate. Again, following the yin-yang principle. For a while, the temperature rises, and falls in a spectrum we know as Summer. As the earth changes in its relationship to the sun, the changes are manifested as cooler temperatures we know as Winter. There are changes within changes, in small cycles such as night and day and longer cycles such as seasons. The cycles change to expand and contract second by second, lasting minutes, hours, days, years and eons. The way our brains process these changes is how we interpret time. However, the ancients, like modern theoretical physicists realized that time is an illusion. It is not time passing; it is our perception to change that gives the illusion of time passing. Our brain is only able to present to the mind a momentary snapshot of life in a linear stream of observation.

---

[19] Perhaps the ultimate release is what we know as the big bang; a hot dense state and BANG. With the bang came the outward movement and creation.

Even our observations are polarized between being present and distracted.

> "We are created in the Tao, and so, therefore, we are the Tao. So, we should be what we are."[20]

Unifying with the principles of nature is unifying with the Tao. The cycle of yin/yang is a rhythm that everything else is automatically unified. Humans have the potential ability to be consciously aware of the choice to be separate from, or connected to nature (Tao). It is only the higher order of animals that break from the Tao as an intention of the mind. The ego is the sub-entity of our spirit that causes us to separate from the Tao and nature as a matter of choice. When a person becomes too distracted within the ego-mind to return to the Tao, they remain disconnected from the Tao. The spirit and Tao unity are our essential nature. This sense of self-awareness is to be 'present' and consciously returning focus to the Tao. This awakening process is meditation. Awake and aware, the Tao cultivator returns to the flow of the Tao which is the Yin/Yang movement.

The Yin and Yang perspective is relevant to the Tao cultivator because it sets the foundation for understanding how the Tao operates as both the source and a way of spiritual discipline. This binary perspective of changing polarity applies to everything. It is an important understanding for developing life strategies. When you factor the Yin-Yang principles of what has happened and

---

[20]Credit for this remark to Alan Watts.

what will happen, you can have more success in shaping your destiny. Knowing that permanence is an illusion, you can accept that change is inevitable.

Conscious awareness as an awakened being is the realization of spirit. Its relationship with the Tao follows the same cosmic rules of the yin/yang flow. Just like the outer cosmos, consciousness follows the yin/yang pattern. Humans experience life and death much like the evolution of the universe. Within the microcosm of a single lifetime experience, there is birth, aging and death. Life and growing are yang. Aging and growing older are becoming Yin. In another perspective, a sperm converges with an egg. The convergent release of the two chromosome chains form together is a cosmic event not much different than the big bang. The process expands all the way to the next convergent point, and the downward cycle begins gaining in amplitude until the next convergent point.

Conception, growth, maturity, aging decline- death. It is the way of all things. There is an inevitability in the yin/yang convergence that cannot be ignored. The time experienced for the process is a subjective illusion. Time is just the quantifying perspective of the change experience.

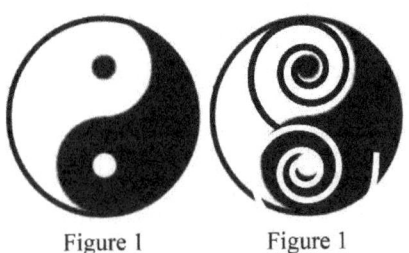

Figure 1   Figure 1

In the Yin-Yang Symbol, figure 1, you can see two main elements. One is black, and one is white. The shapes are sometimes referred to as a "fish" with an "eye." The black shape (yin) is the represented by dark/shade/diminishing, and the white shape is Yang representing increasing, expansion, growth, and increase

Each state will reach a point where it begins to return to its complement. The two states are both complementary and interdependent. The movement or flow will move from abundance to a place of non-abundance. The change and balance are the constantly in movement. The eye of each fish symbolizes the new transition beginning in the old. As the old cycles wane, the new arises. The white fish has a black eye, and the black fish eye is white. Like a pendulum, this creative property flows back and forth seeking balance. One state will eventually become the other. This complementary relationship is the basis for the creation of the universe. I have been told that early Chinese philosophy began with the simple observation of how night becomes day dimming back into the dark. As humans evolved, they noticed patterns all throughout nature. Now with the insights of modern science, these phenomena can be witnessed throughout the universe. Literally the change is spiral in nature. You can see it in the examples of spiral snail shells to hurricanes to a spiral galaxy. At the center of the mystery is the changing state of energy. Perhaps the most significant relationship is that between the spiritual and physical domains.

Here are some ways to see yin/yang in nature:

---

birth becomes death and death converges on birth

Ying Yang

young become old only to return as young

night becomes a day to become a night again

hunger becomes fullness returning to hunger

new becomes used, recycled to become new again

good becomes bad eventually reforming to become good

right becomes left then swing back to the right

shadow gives way to sunlight that diminishes to shadow

beginning reaches an end which immediately begins again

tangible/form becomes intangible/formless becoming tangible/form

matter becomes energy which cycles back to matter

Clarity is the term for realizing how things are. Clarity is seeing the nature of the Tao in life. Through clarity you can observe the nature of life in the Tao. Acceptance is having clarity and abiding with the truth. Going against the nature of the Tao creates stress, tension, and suffering.

Example: When inconvenient weather intervenes with planned outdoor activity and you get upset.

Example: When you become impatient because it is taking too long to make that left turn.

Understanding and acceptance of this fundamental

universal law is a necessary step in developing your wisdom. Resisting, fighting, and denying, only cause internal conflicts. You can learn to unify with the flow of the Tao and find harmony. Striving is going against the nature of something. Harmony is the balance achieved when working with the nature of things.[21]

The wisdom is accepting that creation and change are part of nature. The wisdom is in both acceptance and unifying with nature and its laws. Awareness of this Tao phenomenon and integrating it into your life is an element of attaining the Tao.

What is your relationship with the laws of nature? This may be the first time that you have ever considered such a notion. Tao and the divine are one in the same. When you align your higher consciousness with the Tao, you are attaining the Tao. Attaining the Tao is to be at one with the divine. Why would you not seek that? Your answer will reveal your present relationship to the Tao.

The purpose of this explanation is to set the foundation for understanding the insights, concepts, and virtues that follow in the next chapters of this section. You are encouraged to enrich your perspective of life events and situations by realizing more than one perspective on any given situation that will arise. A multi-perspective view will empower you to increase wisdom.

See the chapter on Harmony in Section Two of this book.

To find harmony, to realize your true destiny, you must unify with the creative law of the universe. You can embrace the concept of change as a creative process. Acceptance and unity with the Tao avoids resistance and creates flow. Unity with the flow is the effortless achievement of unattached action; Wu Wei. *Unattached action* is the ability to detach from ego and ride the flow of change. The convergence point of movement and its creative change are where the effortless action is found. Think of a surfer riding a wave. [22]

To be Sovereign is to reign over the ego mind which resists change. To resist change is to ignore and work against the universal law of creation. To resist the creative power of the universe only creates obstacles to the evolutionary process. This ignorance blocks the potential and possibility of what can be created. Impermanence, change, and creation cannot be stopped. Acceptance of these brings clarity. To accept is to give rise to the possibility.

Learn to see the good within the bad. Learn to see the possibilities where there only seems to be obstacles. Learn to see good where before there was only bad. Learn to find friendship where before there was enmity. A change in perspective will create true wisdom and keep you on your true path.

---

[22] See the chapter on Wu Wei

Ying Yang

Wu Wei

10

EMPTINESS

Thirty spokes join in one hub
In its emptiness is the function of a vehicle
Mix clay to create a container
In its emptiness there is the function of a container
Cut open doors and windows to create a room
In its emptiness, there is the function of a room
Therefore, that which exists is used to create benefit
That which is empty is used to create functionality
Chapter 11, Tao Te Ching

Why Emptiness?

At first look, you may wonder how the concept of emptiness can have any value. After all, by definition, it can be defined as nothingness. If it is true that emptiness is not absolute, then there must be something more to it. Empty and nothing are sometimes subjective and are relevant to the observer.

The Tao principle is that emptiness gives function to form. Alternatively, another way to think about it is, emptiness provides the opportunity for possibility.

23

Emptiness gives function to form

In chapter 11, Lao Tzu shares the concept that emptiness gives functionality to that which is solid.

- It is the hole in the wagon wheel hub that allows an axle to be placed.
- A coffee mug that is a solid cylinder has no space for coffee.
- A room with no doors or windows has little function without a means to enter and exit. It also would have no way for air and light to enter. If a room were solid, there would be no place to dwell and thus have no relevant function.

Emptiness creates the opportunity for possibility

Another perspective you may consider is that an absolute and solid conviction about any subject leaves little room for possibility and discovery. When we can empty our minds from the ego and an entrenched perspective we allow:

- Stillness to create space for awareness
- Awareness to create space for insight

- Spiritual insight and intuition to create space for possibility
- Possibility to create space for the creative energy of the Tao

Stillness – A Meditative State

Another way to view the importance of emptiness is in the concept of stillness. Emptiness of thought and stillness of the mind is a detached state of being. Detached observation is to be observant of the incessant mind-stream of thinking. Within the stillness, in that gap between the episodes of thinking, you can gain insight. Stillness is the residence of the spiritual self or the silent witness. A mind that is still is quiet. This transcended state is the concentration of attention outside of the voice of the ego. It is focused and observing yet empty of reactive judgment. In this space awaits the potential for creativity and insight. It is in the emptiness between thought, "the gap" where wisdom can guide choices. Stillness is a prerequisite for sovereignty.[24]

Consider this; who is it that is observing the mind? That alone should give you pause. This observer is pure consciousness. Realization of that essence of being, that part of you that observes, is the object of meditation. This is your spiritual core; observing and realizing what is crossing over the mind, yet free from it. This is true self-awareness. When you sit in stillness you return to calm abiding (meditative state).

Creative potential remains unknown when the mind is busy with too much activity. Incessant thinking becomes a form of distraction. As the Sovereign, the ruler of your inner-kingdom, you hold the potential for creative power. Insight and wisdom are waiting and can only be attained when the mind is still and has clarity.

Each of us has enormous potential waiting in the stillness. When thinking arises, it creates the reality we dwell in. Stillness brings patience and clarity. Then choices can be guided by wisdom to take the right action.

The Tao cultivator cannot begin working on self-control until he or she has developed enough skill to return often to the stillness of the meditative state. Learning to meditate is devotion. It is difficult because it requires self-discipline. The spirit (true self) must use discipline over the ego-self. Like anything else, the more you practice, the better you

---

[24] See chapter 4, Meditation and Mindfulness, the section on "Stillness"

get. Being Sovereign is to empty the heart and mind of ego hunger so that you create the space for awareness.

Emptiness

11

WU WEI

"No matter what it is you do, there is always a way to do it that is effective, effortless, and enjoyable at the deepest level. This is the true meaning of Wu Wei." Derek Lin[25]

Another important principle of sovereignty is Wu Wei.

Typically, the term "wu wei" is translated as non-doing. However, to think that it means to do nothing is just a superficial understanding. The deeper insight is *"unattached action."* There are several chapters devoted to wu wei, and each has a unique and important perspective.

If you spend enough time with Tao studies, you will at some point hear the term "accomplish more by doing less." This chapter illuminates the principles of Wu Wei and the ego traits to corrupt sovereignty.

---

[25] From the Tao of Happiness, Derek Lin, The Tao of Happiness: Stories from *Chuang Tzu* for Your Spiritual Journey

UNATTACHED ACTION

The softest things of the world
Override the hardest things of the world
That which has no substance
Enters into that which has no openings
From this I know the benefits of unattached actions
The teaching without words
The benefits of actions without attachment
Are rarely matched in the world
Chapter 43, Tao Te Ching

The foundation of Wu Wei is *unattached action*. This foundation principle involves several components. In chapter 43, Lao Tzu explains how softness overcomes hardness. In the physical world water is soft to the touch but will wear away stone over time. Water penetrates stone and weakens it. This process will eventually change rock and stone to sand. The most obvious example of this can be seen by looking at the Grand Canyon. Also, when you walk along a beach, you can feel the soft sand that was once solid hard rock. Following the Tao is following nature. In nature water does not have an agenda to wear away the rock, it is not attached to the outcome of creating sand, it just does what it does effortlessly. So, another principle of wu wei is not to get caught up in the ego's attachment to outcome.

Attachment to Outcome

The principle of detached action is another way of looking

at how water wears down hard rock. Water is just water and has no attachment to outcome. The sages have instructed us to be like the Tao, so in this case, we are asked to be like water.

When you can be mindful of attachment, you choose an action that is not dependent on a specific outcome. This important principle forms the bedrock for

---

"giving without expectation"

"producing without possessing"

"and nurtures without domination"

Excerpt from Chapter 10, Tao Te Ching

Water does not benefit the world with the expectation of a reward, and neither should we. The ego always takes action with the expectation of some benefit to itself. This principle of unattached action is important in developing good relationships. You cannot build trust if you are only doing something because you are only concerned with what's in it for yourself. This type of exploitation will have a karmic outcome that you will not enjoy.

Striving

Another way of defining wu wei is action without striving. Attachment to outcome sets up the ego state of striving. Striving is defined as making a struggle, to make a vigorous exertion, to achieve or obtain something. Other features to note are that striving creates friction and uses much energy. It is working against the flow, experiencing resistance, to stubbornly pursuing something even when it does not make sense.

Without going out the door, know the world

Without peering out the window, see the Heavenly Tao

The further one goes

The less one knows

Therefore the sage knows without going

Names without seeing

Achieves without striving.

Chapter 47, Tao Te Ching

Striving is the action of ego. It is like swimming upstream, racing against the wind or pushing against an immovable object. Even if eventually you realize achievement, the effort will be too costly.

Accomplishing More by Doing Less

The Tao is constant in non-action

Yet there is nothing it does not do.

If the sovereign can hold on to this

All things transform themselves

Transformed, yet wishing to achieve

I shall restrain them with the simplicity of the nameless

They shall be without desire

Without desire, using stillness

The world shall steady itself

Chapter 37, Tao Te Ching

Opposite to striving is "effortless achievement." Like water effortlessly created the grand-canyon or the beautiful beach, you too can reach your goals by going with the flow of the Tao.

Effortless achievement involves simplicity. When you remove the ego influence from your perspective, simplicity becomes the way. Simplicity and effortlessness complement each other. The ego can get caught up in all sorts of crazy expectations driven by desire. Cleverness and complexity are a couple of common traps that make goal achievement much harder. Desire traits such as greed, lust, and vanity are a couple more distractions that will cause an attachment to outcome.

Controlling the ego is controlling desire. Desire can be a material gain, or it can be a form of vanity. Through the stillness of the meditative mind, you can get to the root of your desire that causes striving. *You will realize success in a way that is with minimum effort and without striving.*

To apply wu wei as a living strategy requires being skilled in detached observation. In this state, you can be mindful and pay attention to your actions in the present moment. You can call it a situational awareness. Become aware of a strong momentum that you may have as you strive to complete some ego driven outcome. The ego trying as hard as it can to get what it wants is moving against the flow. Where in wu wei you have the presence of mind to be detached from that desire driven outcome. Let simplicity and virtue guide you. Like water, you softly, patiently penetrate that striving pursuit and listen to your wisdom. When you can accomplish this, effortless achievement will become a very powerful tool.

Wu Wei is more than just a concept; it is a state of being. It is a state of being unified with the Tao.

Emptiness

"Because Tao is the total spontaneity of all things,

so it can do everything by doing nothing."

Fung Yu-Lan[26]

The Tao spontaneously creates without effort or agenda. Cultivating Wu Wei has to become a way of life. This state of being is a kind of connected-consciousness. Maybe you have seen the phenomena but not recognized it for what it is. Some popular descriptions might be "in the zone" or "in the flow." Meditation and mindfulness practice is how to develop the skill of being present and mindful of striving and attachment to outcome.

As the Sovereign, being self-aware, you can control the ego-choice from fixating on the outcome. Through life experience you gain wisdom, but you must have the discipline and willpower to listen to it and choose the right action; the unattached action. Let virtue guide your choices and actions.

---

[26] 3Fung Yu-Lan 1895-1990; was a Chinese philosopher, author of Chuang-Tzu, a translation and interpretation of Chuang- Tzu's writings.

SECTION Two– A Study of Virtue

Section Two

A Study of Virtue

"...Thus those who follow the Tao are with the Tao
Those who follow virtue are with virtue
Those who follow loss are with loss
Those who are with the Tao, the Tao is pleased to have them.
Those who are true to virtue, virtue is pleased to have them
Those who are with loss, loss is also pleased to have them..."
Chapter 23, verses 7-12, Tao Te Ching

There is a name for people who have devoted a lifetime cultivating the Tao and attaining sovereignty. They are called Sages. Accumulating virtue is the mastery of gaining power through implementing virtue as a way of life. However, the power they gain is not power in the usual sense. What they gain is very special. It is called inherent power. Inherent power is necessary for realizing sovereignty.

Cultivating sovereignty takes a lifetime of accumulating virtue. This section is a study in Tao virtues and how you can discover those inherent powers.

Some of the virtues discussed in this section do not directly appear in the Tao Te Ching. However, these virtues become self-evident as you study and practice the way of virtue. A good place to begin is the virtues of The Three Treasures.

Living the Tao is to be mindful and to practice the way of virtue in everyday life. Through daily practice, you will gain experience that will enable you to realize the wisdom inherent in each virtue. The inherent powers of these virtues and lay the foundation for real success in life as you face its inevitable challenges. Virtue is real power. The way of virtue is the way of the Sovereign

12

THE THREE TREASURES

Everyone in the world calls my Tao great
As if it is beyond compare
It is only because of its greatness
That it seems beyond compare
If it can be compared
It would already be insignificant long ago
I have three treasures
I hold on to them and protect them
The first is called compassion
The second conservation
The third called not daring to be ahead in the world
Compassionate, thus able to have true courage
Conserving, thus able to reach widely
Not daring to be ahead in the world
Thus able to assume leadership
Now if one has courage but discards compassion
Reaches widely but discards conservation
Goes ahead but discards being behind
Then death
If one fights with compassion, then victory
With defense, then security
Heaven shall save them
And with compassion guard them
Chapter 67, Tao Te Ching

It is understandable why Lao Tzu called these three virtues as treasures that he holds on to and protects. These three virtues are applicable in every aspect of life.

The three treasures create a three-way complementary relationship with each other. Each one gives true context for the other two.

Compassion harmonizes with Conservation and Humility

Conservation harmonizes with Humility and Compassion

Humility harmonizes with Compassion and Conservation

If you are just beginning your conscious effort of cultivating, start with these three. Use these three as your moral compass in everyday life. When you have used them long enough, they will become second nature as you develop your Tao strategies for solving problems. On a personal note, I consider these three so important that you could spend the rest of your life cultivating just these three. It is worth the effort for yourself as well as the rest of the world.

Becoming present is to return from striving in the world. The present moment is where you live. By being present you can follow your true path. Consider The Three Treasures very significant guides for the road home. Spiritually speaking, home is a state of being. It is one of tranquility stillness and sanctuary. The path back home is very difficult when you do not follow the way of virtue. Escaping the suffering of ego is impossible without following the path of virtue. Cultivating sovereignty through the practice of virtue is the journey back home.

Compassion

13

COMPASSION

"...I have three treasures
I hold on to them and protect them
The first is called compassion..."
Chapter 67, verses 7,8, and 9, Tao Te Ching

Compassion is a conviction of love and kindness for another being. It is a virtue that comes from the heart. The Sovereign, as a spiritual being, recognizes the spirit in other living beings. Note that the Sovereign does not discriminate in their recognition of other living beings. As human beings, we share the planet with a very large number of other beings, who just happen to dwell in different bodies. The Tao is not exclusive to humans, and an argument can be made that plenty of beings in the animal world are closer in unity with nature (Tao) than humanity. However, at least for the beginner on the path, compassion (loving kindness) for other humans is a useful place to begin.

Another aspect of compassion to consider is the state of being indifferent. Indifference is defined as having lack of interest or concern. People tend to stay in their comfort zones and avoid conflict. However, as a people we are all connected. You don't have to save the world, but you can pay attention to the world close around you. You know the old saying "what goes around comes around," which is a colloquial way of remembering how karma plays a role in all our lives. Sooner or later, the moment will come when you will need someone's help. And in that moment when you need caring or compassion most, you could find yourself out in the cold.

As discussed earlier, true virtues have inherent powers. The inherent power of compassion is true courage. [27]

"...compassionate, thus able to have true courage..."

Chapter 67, verse 12, Tao Te Ching

Courage is sometimes confused with bravado or showing off by doing something dangerous. An example of courage by virtue of compassion can be seen when a mother comes to the defense of her child. It is not just a human attribute. The same compassionate courage can be seen throughout nature. Just as a human mother will not hesitate to face great odds against her, mother in nature will do the same. The internet is full of videos showing animal mothers protecting their young against dangerous predators. The inherent power of compassion is not limited to mothers. You too can practice compassion (loving kindness, caring) and realize the power of true courage.

"...If one fights with compassion, then victory

With defense, then security

Heaven shall save them

And with compassion guard them..."

---

[27] See the Chapter True Courage, Chapter 16 for clarity on courage vs bravery

Compassion Instead of Needing to Win (or be right)

"...So when evenly matched armies meet

The side that is compassionate shall win..."

Chapter 69, Verses 9 & 10, Tao Te Ching

The ego needs to win, and to be right. To achieve a goal or to be victorious can cause the best of us to forget compassion at a moment where it might be needed most. Opposing views or needs often set the stage for conflict. The alternative to the self-righteous stance of having to be right or win is to step back and consider the situation from a point of compassion.

The Tao cultivator who practices sovereignty remembers the wisdom of not contending. They can remain detached from the ego's need of having to be right. By softening the perspective and intention, compassion can lead the way to equanimity between parties. It can open the door to mutual understanding, compromise, and friendship. Compromise is the result of putting the need to be right aside and consider compassion for those who need it.

When your efforts are grounded in the compassion of helping someone outside of yourself courage will empower you to stick with the effort and to endure.

There is no true victory in crushing your opponent with no consideration of compassion. The Sovereign approaches conflict armed with compassion so that real victory is possible for both sides.

14

CONSERVATION

"...the second is called conservation..." verse 10
"...conserving thus able to able to reach widely..." verse 13
Chapter 67, Tao Te Ching

Conservation is the second of the three treasures. To conserve is to use and manage resources wisely. Conservation as a virtuous principle is to wisely preserve the important sources and resources so that balance and harmony can be maintained for prosperity. Mindful and aware of how the ego can interfere and disrupt harmony is a key factor in maintaining sovereignty. The adherence to this virtue begins with paying attention to conserving resources.

Conserving Your Resources

Conserving your resources so you don't run out of the essentials in life should be a no-brainer. However, the experience of running out and depleting resources happens to so many of us that it deserves a close examination. The simple answer is that when a person is absorbed in the ego state of mind they suffer from both distraction and illusion. So often the ego is so busy striving to fulfill a variety of desires that it is not paying to how fast resources are being depleted. It is so busy coping with problems that it is unaware or uncaring that resources are not being replenished. The other issue is living under the illusion of "it can't happen to me."

The solution is conservation. Even if you can recognize the wisdom of this virtue, being able to implement it can be difficult if you are too distracted. Again, meditation and mindfulness are key skills to gain awareness of the reality of circumstances. It comes down to a choice between wisdom or ignorance. The true self is aligned with virtue and wisdom. The ego is absorbed in self-serving ignorance. When you have cultivated self-discipline (sovereignty), you can supersede ego's ignorance and take the right action. That choice will be picked up by and played out through karma.

Want vs. Need

This focus on conservation is a good opportunity to look at the dilemma of want vs. need. Understanding the difference is a straightforward concept. However, so many of us fail at it. Moderation is a good management tool for reaching a balance between what you want and what you need. The problem occurs when the ego confuses the two. Being narcissistic by nature, it has the illusion that everything it wants is a need. The true self can rise above narcissism and be honest and accurate about what's needed. This can help conserve resources in a big way. However, depriving yourself of too much can create a sense of imbalance. The simple wisdom is to take care of what you need first, then, with care and caution consider what you want and why you want it.

Tangible Resources

Resources follow the dichotomy of the Tao like everything else. There are both tangible and non-tangible resources. When you lose the tangible resources, such as food, and shelter you can find yourself on rock bottom. These are true needs that must be conserved or you may end up becoming dependent upon those who have compassion and are willing to share. Tangible resources like food, water, and shelter are necessary to sustain life. In our society, our ability to obtain these is often determined by financial resources or money. Money in its tangible form is a necessary resource of very high importance for sustainability. If you have no money, it is very difficult to purchase the necessities of life. So, it is self-evident that having enough money on a continuous basis is a wise strategy. It is easy to conclude that you should make sure to conserve your financial resources so that you do not cause yourself suffering. It is much easier to sustain a state of mental and emotional harmony when you have enough of the basics.

Intangible Resources

Some resources are important yet do not have a physical form. Currency and coinage are physical forms of money. Credit on the other hand, is an intangible resource. There are other forms of intangible resources that are important to conserve such as good relations, friendship, and trust. One important way of conserving good relations is to be a team player and be cooperative.

Cooperation is very important when you need to accomplish something where a group or groups are involved. Balance and harmony are key traits to maintaining relationships with others in your social network. The Sovereign will pay close attention to familial relationships. Family relationships can and should be at the top of your list of areas to conserve. Without this, your most important network will become dysfunctional.

Conservation of Spirit (Constancy)[28]

Conservation of spirit is one of the highest virtues. Returning to presence as a spiritual being is referred to as constancy. Conservation of spirit empowers you to manage the ego and desire so that you do not deplete your resources. As always it comes back to conservation of spirit to be mindful of choices. Choosing actions that conserve both intangible and tangible assets is key to longevity and avoiding suffering and death.

Perhaps the most important resource to conserve is "presence." Being present is being self-aware. Self-awareness is the awakened state from which spirit rules over the ego. It may be the most important use of conservation because without being sovereign you will not be able to control the ego. Through the conservation of spirit you will be able to conserve your physical presence. Thus, your body is the vehicle for having the physical experience. The degree of success that you achieve in maintaining your physical body is directly proportional to the quality of your life. Your body is the ultimate physical resource. Without a body you cannot experience life and your spiritual evolution comes to a stop. When you deplete its ability to sustain itself you die and the experience ends. The most important act of conservation in the physical is to take care of your body. The bottom line is that you must conserve the mind – body – spirit relationship by controlling the ego.

The self-destruction of your body comes from internal disharmony. So, you can begin to understand how the spiritual conservation is extremely important. Your mind is

---

[28] See the Chapter on Constancy and Clarity

the quantum processor between spirit and physical, so what happens in the mind will manifest in the physical.

It Is Not Just About You

Remember, our actions are like ripples in a pond. We are all connected. Your ignorance can affect so many. When you deplete your spiritual awareness and make selfish choices the result can affect others. When you waste your life, others must sacrifice some of their resources to help you start over. Those with compassion are willing to help. However, it is important to know that compassion from others can have a limit. If you hit bottom and have a chance to start over, you must use the gift of compassion from others to help yourself return to harmony. Gratitude can go a long way for continued assistance.

The penalty for continuing to be a prisoner of ego and self-serving narcissism is dealt out by karma. Karma sometimes called "the great executioner," does not play favorites. Any notion of "it cannot happen to me" will be crushed. Karma is the result of your own ignorant choices. *The results of your actions can be problematic for others around you. Hopefully, you will never have to observe how your stupid mistakes have hurt the people you care for.* You must be honest with yourself and realized how your actions can play out.

Conservation is a virtue that the Sovereign works at to build wisdom. You must be mindful of your resources and keep harmony in your life. Work on ego traits such as attachments and narcissism and replace them with virtue. Recognize ignorance for what it is and choose wisdom. Conserve your identity as a spiritual being by devoting to the practice of meditation and mindfulness. Work on being the Sovereign.

Conservation

Humility

15

HUMILITY

"...I have three treasures
I hold on to them and protect them
The first is called compassion
The second is called conservation
The third is called not getting ahead in the world..."
Chapter 67, Verses 7 – 11, Tao Te Ching

Verse 11, *"the third is called not getting ahead in the world,"* is stating the virtue of humility. *"Getting ahead in the world"* is the antithesis of humility.

It is:

- Self-Promotion
- Self- Gain
- Striving to Profit at the expense of others

Sometimes it is necessary to use these traits in everyday life. However, when they are used to exploit or take unnecessary advantage of others it becomes problematic. This action is only satisfying ego desire. These traits can even be seen in nature. Without the virtue of humility, the ego will use them to fulfill its narcissistic desire. Use virtue to guide yourself to clarity. These are just a few ego traits. If you become mindful of this trait, you will notice others that arise in various situations.

Just like in practicing the virtue of conservation you should be mindful of want vs. need.[29]

In our society, the virtue of "not getting ahead in the world" is known as humility. The ego is always putting itself first. This virtue, humility, is a complementary of compassion and conservation. In conserving spirit, you have transcended the self-important or self-promoting aspect of ego. Compassion is the true self (spirit) being sympathetic, empathetic, and caring for the suffering and wellbeing of others. The joining of compassion and conserving, returning and conserving of the true self, and being selfless, opens the door to a state of non-self-importance. Humility is not putting your-self first.

As the Sovereign cultivator gains more and more control of ego, the need for self-importance begins to subside. Neediness is a core principle of the ego-self. The need to have attention, to be seen as the best, to strive to always to be ahead [of everyone else] is how the ego spends its life. Seeking "to get ahead in the world."[30]

Like the hub of a wagon wheel, being empty of ego, humility gives function to so many other principles and virtues of the Tao. Here are some relevant verses from the Tao Te Ching to contemplate:

Tao Te Ching Chapter 8...

"...The highest goodness resembles water,

---

[29] See the Chapter 14; Conservation (previous chapter). It is a discussion wants vs. needs.

[30] Humility is being like water and seeking the low places. (Chapter 8, Tao Te Ching)

Humility

Water benefits myriad things without contention

It stays in places that people dislike

Therefore, it is similar to the Tao..."

Chapter 22, verses 3-11 "....be low and become filled

Be worn out and become renewed

Have little and receive

Have much and be confused

Therefore the sages hold to the one as an example for the world

Without flaunting themselves, they are seen clearly

Without presuming themselves, and are distinguished

Without praising themselves, and so have merit

Without boasting about themselves and so are lasting..."

Chapter 28, verses 9-11"...The eternal virtue does not deviate

Return to the state of the boundless

Know the honor, hold the humility..."

Chapter 39, verses 15-16 "...The honored uses the lowly as a basis

The higher uses the lower as a foundation..."

Chapter 66, verses 1-5, "...Rivers and oceans can be the kings of a hundred valleys

Because of their goodness in staying low

So, they can be kings of a hundred valleys

Thus if sages wish to be over people

They must speak humbly to them..."

Humility opens the mystic door to the insight that those who are blinded by ego, desire, and self-importance cannot see or comprehend the power of humility. Humility is the gateway to the Tao. Humility enables so many other virtues such as patience, acceptance, and simplicity.

The low places, places of humility, are where nature deposits its treasure. Humility is where the Sovereign cultivates the wisdom of the Tao. The ego, always seeking the highest (to be seen, to get the most, to be the best, to stand out), moves away from where the Tao will hand out its rewards.

In personal relationships, humility opens the door for non-contention. When you are not trying to take advantage of, or get the best of other, you will find friendship.

Chapter 22, Verse 12 "...because they do not contend

the world cannot contend with them..."

Let's have a moment of truth. Take an honest look at your life and at your relationships and see where you can improve on the virtue of humility.

> • *How often do you feel like you must win, or be the best?*
> • *How often do you feel that you must be the one who is right?*
> • *How important is it to you to better than everyone else?*
> • *When was the last time you accepted a lowly and menial task to help someone else?*
> • *How often do you feel that you deserve more?*
> • *How often has someone you know told you that you complain too much?*
> • *Are you arrogant?*
> • *Do you relate humility as a kind of ignorance?*
> • *What tasks have you been asked to do, but you feel they are beneath you?*
> • *Have you thought about pretending humility so that people will admire you?*

Moreover, the ultimate question, how hard is it for you to practice true humility?

Without humility, compassion is empty. Without humility, conservation is very difficult to practice. Without humility, there is no sovereignty.

Humility

Humility

16

TRUE COURAGE

"...I have three treasures
I hold on to them and protect them
The first is called compassion
The second is called conservation
The third is called not daring to get ahead in the world
Compassionate, thus able to have courage
Conserving, thus able to reach widely
Not daring to get ahead in the world
Thus able to assume leadership
Now if one has courage but discards compassion
Reaches widely but discards conservation
Goes ahead but discards being behind
Then death...!"
Chapter 67, verses 7 – 19, Tao Te Ching.

True Courage vs. Bravery

True courage is the inherent power of compassion. And although we, many times, use the words courage and bravery to mean the same thing, in the context of the Tao virtue, they are different.

Courage is thought to be the ability to face difficulty, danger, and pain. This definition could also be applied to the word bravery, boldness, or guts as well. On a whole, we use them interchangeably.

The distinction in Tao study can be found in the examination of the intention or mindset for how and why one faces danger and difficulty. One intention is to serve the self; the other is to serve something other than self. True courage is found through compassion and serving someone or something other than your specific need or point of view.

If you initiate an internet search for symbols of courage, you will see many images of the lion. The lion is a symbol of both power and true courage.

To understand how compassion creates true courage, think of how the mothers or parents of many species will face great danger or difficulty to protect their young. Human parents will endure years of hardship and sacrifice to enable their children to have a good life. In nature, it is easy to see how mothers can be ferocious when their cubs are threatened. Every year we hear in the news how a mother bear attacked hikers or campers who came too close to the cubs.

Another perspective of how people will exhibit true courage for something other than their wellbeing can be seen when they serve their team, their country, or even humanity. Courage and sacrifice for the greater good are the elements of virtue that gives us true courage.

Then there is bravery. I use bravery as a comprehensive word to represent the different actions where one faces difficulty, adversity, danger, and sacrifice because of self-gain. Greed, avarice, vanity, anger, and vengeance are just a few the ego's motivating factors that can cause people to face danger or sacrifice one thing to get another. Some examples might be a bank robber who just wants to be rich. Alternatively, it might be swindling older people out of their money. In both situations, the perpetrator faces challenges and the danger of getting caught, yet you can see the motivations for self-gain.

Sometimes a person's ego can be so self-convincing to the degree that they draw others into their dangerous plight because they are convinced that their idea will save the day. It gives credence to the saying "the road to hell is paved with good intentions." It is still just a matter of a self-serving mindset for the ego or even collective ego.

Seemingly good ideas can become a self-serving ideology masked under the name of religion.

If you are still not convinced, try considering what Lao Tzu says in verses 16 and 19,

> *verse 16 "...Now if one has courage but discards compassion..."*

> *verse 19 ... "...then death..."*

"Death" can be both a metaphor for self-destruction and loss, or it can be literal. Taking dangerous chances because of ego pursuits can end in death. Taking chances with financial resources because of greed can result in a great financial loss.

Once again, you can see how important it is to be mindfully aware of the mind and the ego's influence over intentions. In those moments of choice, you must know what you are doing and why, otherwise the chance you are taking will not be based on true courage and will end badly for all involved.

To step out of your comfort zone in order to help someone takes courage. In this way, courage becomes a virtue and karma will reflect your true intention. Today and every day the opportunity for courage will present itself. It might be helping someone stand up to a bully. It may be a chance to push back on bigotry or racism. You may be called on to sacrifice something important to you so that someone else gets what they really need. A moment of truth will present itself that offers you a chance to have the courage to move beyond judgment and be compassionate. Be aware if you are doing it because you will look good and be famous. Are you doing it to help stop someone's suffering?

You will have the choice to be safely indifferent to someone in need or to have the courage to do the right thing. I hope for karma's sake that you make the right choice. I guarantee you that someone in your future will need for you to have true courage and act selflessly.

Inherent Power of True Courage

Because of her true courage, she was able to inspire the workforce to achieve its goal in record time while keeping morale high.

When a leader and its group have a common goal, the leader can use compassion to lead the workforce. Putting her ego-agenda aside and addressing the concerns of the workers raise the spirit of the workforce/team. They, in turn, will sacrifice and give extra effort for victory because they will be acting with compassion for those who stand to benefit from their efforts. These beneficiaries can be the other workers and the consumer.[31]

On the other hand, when the leader can be only focused on the result and uses coercion, manipulation, and trickery and forces the effort without compassion, then there will be a failure or at best, limited success. Enmity to the leader will sour any success and people will not want to follow them in the future.

True courage is knowing the "two standards"[32] and choosing the right action? Compassionate courage is a virtue of sovereignty. Practice often.

---

[31] See the chapter on Compassion

[32] The two standards are virtue and ego traits. See Chapter 6 Mystic Virtue

Constancy - Clarity

17

CONSTANCY AND CLARITY

Attain the ultimate emptiness
Hold on to the truest tranquility
The myriad things are all active
I therefore watch their return
Everything flourishes, each returns to its root
Returning to the root is called tranquility
Tranquility is called returning to one's nature
Returning to one's nature is called constancy
Knowing constancy is called clarity
Not knowing constancy, one recklessly causes trouble
Knowing constancy is acceptance
Acceptance is impartiality
Impartiality is sovereign
Sovereign is Heaven
Heaven is Tao
Tao is eternal
The self is no more, without danger
Chapter 16, Tao Te Ching

Constancy is a necessary element of cultivating sovereignty. In this context, we can define constancy as a faithful return to the stillness of the Tao. What does this mean?

There are several references throughout the Tao Te Ching about returning to, and being in, a meditative state. The meditative state can be thought of as pure awareness within the stillness of the mind. In this stillness, empty of mind movement is tranquility. In tranquility is you will discover your true nature. Your true nature is being. Stillness is being and being is spirit.

Returning

The physical experience of life requires that we go forth and work to sustain our presence in the physical realm. As we engage our world we use our mind to think.

"...The myriad things are all active..." (verse 3)

Stillness awaits you in the silence between episodes of thinking. In stillness, you are at one with the Tao. This is returning. You are returning from the mental movement of thoughts and thinking to the stillness of pure consciousness and pure being. It is a return from ignorance to wisdom, from avarice to virtue, and from narcissism to altruism to realize and maintain harmony. Harmony leads to tranquility.

"...I therefore watch their return

Everything flourishes, each returns to its root..."
(verses 4 - 5)

This action is consistent with the yin-yang principle. All things go and all things return. All creatures live their lives and then return to the Tao. Spiritually, we move out into the world in thought, and then we must return to the stillness of the Tao. All things return to their root. This is an especially important insight for the Tao cultivator.

Tranquility is realized when you have moved beyond the thoughts (transcended) that drive you crazy and that create problems. In the dichotomy of Taoism, it can be thought of as heaven and earth. Alternatively, spiritual and physical. Our source, or root, is our spiritual connection to the source (The Tao). To live at one with the Tao is to return to it by becoming still.

As a physical living being, we must engage in the physical aspects of living. Food, shelter, and thriving are daily activities that keep our physical presence in a sustained manner. However, we must return to the spirit to maintain harmony. The harmony is a balance between spiritual and physical, being and doing, and your true nature and ego.

The meditative state is pure being, and mindfulness is the non-judgmental view of what you are thinking. Cultivating harmony is continuously returning to spiritual awareness and the tranquility of calm-abiding. It is reflected in the principle of yin-yang. Yin is/spiritual, and yang is physical/action. This faithful return to spirit and oneness with the stillness of the Tao is constancy.

Clarity

Spiritual clarity is seeing things as they are without the ambiguity created by the ego. Narcissistic traits and a self-serving agenda always taint the ego perspective. The ego is unable to see the underlying reality because its nature is often caught up in illusion.

"...Returning to one's nature is called constancy

Knowing constancy is called clarity

Not knowing constancy, one recklessly causes trouble..." verses 8-10

When the ego has too much control over decision making and choices trouble and suffering ensue. The ego abhors wisdom and will default to whatever desire happens to be prevailing. It will ignore the wise choice as it tries to fulfill its lust. Ignoring wisdom and following ignorance will recklessly cause trouble for itself and others.

When you have transcended the ego and have returned to spirit, you use discernment to see reality as it is. Detached from ego, you will be able to accept reality and take the right action accordingly.[33] Rather than being controlled by reactions and perception of the ego, the choices you make, the steps you take are in unity with the Tao. Wise choices create harmony.[34] Harmony means more successes and less suffering. Harmony is the nature of the Tao. Harmony sustains longevity. With the self-discipline of the sovereign spirit holding the ego under control your path is less fraught with the dangers of bad choices.

"Knowing constancy is acceptance

Acceptance is impartiality

Impartiality is sovereign

[33] See the chapter on Acceptance

[34] See the chapter on Harmony

Sovereign is Heaven

Heaven is Tao

Tao is eternal

The self is no more, without danger..."

verses 10 - 16

The inherent powers of constancy are clarity and acceptance. Because of the power of constancy you will be able to see things as they are and to practice acceptance. By virtue of sovereignty you can experience a longer life with more harmony. This is the way of Sovereignty. This is the Tao.

Constancy - Clarity

Acceptance

18

ACCEPTANCE

"Not knowing constancy, one recklessly causes trouble
Knowing constancy is acceptance
Acceptance is impartiality
Impartiality is Sovereign
Sovereign is Heaven
Heaven is Tao
Tao is eternal
The self is no more, without danger"
Chapter 16, Verses 10 – 17, Tao Te Ching

Acceptance begins in the present moment. It is consent or permission given by the true self to accept the reality of the present moment. Unity with the Tao can only occur when you can accept what is happening. Another perspective of acceptance is to consider its opposites. Attitudes of denial, disagreement, contending, and dissension are aspects of the ego which reject reality and seek the illusion that it feels entitled to have.

Acceptance is a gateway virtue unlocking the implementation of other virtues such as honesty, cooperation, patience, wisdom, contentment, detachment, gratitude, and simplicity.

Three Options for Acceptance

My experience with acceptance is that there are three responses to what happens to us. You can do nothing, try to change it, or move it or yourself away.

1. Accept that it has or is happening. Be patient and realize that no action is required (the action of no action).

2. Accept that it has happened or is happening. See if you can change:

   A. The conditions that give rise to the situation

   B. Your perspective on the situation

   C. Your reaction to the situation

3. Accept that it has happened or is happening and move or remove:

   A. Move away from the situation.

   B. Remove the conditions that create the problem/situation.

   C. Remove yourself from the situation.

Self-Honesty

Honesty is a form of acceptance where we truthfully define our relationship with reality. Self-honesty is a transcended state where we have risen above the deceptions of the ego and accept our relationship with the present moment. Without self-honesty we stay attached to the illusions of the ego. Self-honesty is a first step in the study of the virtue of acceptance. If you can observe your self-talk you will realize the aspects of selves (ego and spirit) talking to each other. All sorts of self-deception can occur when the ego, the opposite of sovereignty, is in charge. Self-honesty is a virtue of the true self. Self-honest empowers you to accept the truth of how you got to where you are at this moment of your life. Good or bad this is the destiny that you have created. To evolve spiritually, you must practice self-honesty to the best of your ability. It is not always easy. It is a lifelong practice to be cultivated. Sometimes it is difficult understanding what the truth is. You will find your self-truth through meditative self-reflection and acceptance.

The nature of acceptance is not to deny reality. If you are a victim in some way, then you do not have to accept the abuse. You do have to accept the reality of what is happening to find a solution.

Accepting reality can be very hard to do because it involves admitting our mistakes. However, you cannot turn mistakes into wisdom until you accept them and learn not to repeat them. There are times when the reality is too painful or too uncomfortable to accept. You can live under the illusion that the problem or situation is not there, but there is the chance that it will not go away on its own. Taking ownership of your actions is a necessary form of acceptance that is required for self-improvement.

Sovereign cultivators know the wisdom in resolving a problem while it is still small and manageable rather than deny the problem until it grows into a much larger possible impossible situation and becomes impossible to resolve.

Bias Confirmation

It is in our nature to seek confirmation that we are in fact seeing the truth. It is how we substantiate what we already believe. So, the wisdom is to challenge your views and investigate why you feel the way you do with an open and honest perspective. The question becomes one of asking if your view is virtuous in its essence or self-serving in an inappropriate way. When reflecting upon your views, you can recognize any ego (self-serving) bias that is not spiritual. It is also important to realize if the bias is based on an intention or outcome that rewards the ego with some desire fulfillment. Most spiritual paths have a set of spiritual guidelines to follow. In your moment of choice, you can weigh the perceived truth against these guidelines to see if they are virtuous or not. Whether you adhere to The Ten Commandments, The Eightfold Path, or The Three Treasures, be mindful of the influence of ego steering you away from the true path.

Mindfulness affords the opportunity to become aware of your response to situations that arise in the present moment. If you are paying attention you can choose to accept the reality of a given situation and then try one of the three options (wait it out, change it, remove it).

A complement to acceptance is wisdom. Accepting the reality of a situation can open the door to taking the right action. The right action is found by when you consider your life experience and then implement virtuous solutions. Wisdom is gained by learning from past mistakes and knowing what *not to do* again. Virtuous solutions initiate a positive cause and effect that will create a better destiny in the future.

The result of non-acceptance is denial. By not accepting reality you become entrapped in a false hope that becomes a self-created prison. Non-acceptance brings about striving and resistance which cause stress. [35]

Acceptance is recognition of your relationship with karma. When you recognize your part in the causation, you can choose a different course of action that has the desired result. Even when the situation was caused by others, the way you react will be creating karma. Recognition is a key factor in taking ownership of your current future destiny.

Be Like Water

The pride of the ego can also create resistance because of negative traits such as embarrassment, humiliation, defiance, anger, and many others. This stress creates friction when you go against the natural flow of reality. The Tao teachings call for us to be like water and move effortlessly around obstacles. It advises us to be soft, flexible, and to bend when conditions are stormy. Stiffness and rigidity lead to failure. Getting stuck in the resentment of what has happened delays the ability to flow around the obstacle.

---

[35] See more about striving and accomplishing more by doing less in Chapter 10 Wu Wei

> *"...that which is soft and yielding*
>
> *is the follower of life*
>
> *Therefore, an inflexible army will not win*
>
> *A strong tree will be cut down*
>
> *The big and forceful occupy a lowly position*
>
> *While the soft and pliant occupy a higher place"*
>
> *Chapter 76, Verses 7 - 11, Tao Te Ching*

Attachment

Attachment is the inverse of acceptance. Non-acceptance is an attitude of attachment to ego principles. The ego needs to be seen by others as being the victor, of being right, of looking good, of being seen as successful, etc. When the ego takes a hard stand, becomes entrenched and demonstrates an inflexible perspective it prevents wisdom from providing true success. Being stubborn is not a virtue, being humble and open minded is. Time and history prove that this attitude cannot stand. The soft and flexible will endure long after the hard, stiff, and the dead are gone.

Investigate

How does one know what to accept and what is true? I encourage you to investigate and seek clarity. The ego is tricky and can bend the teachings of the Tao into false self-serving virtue. Yet the spirit will see ego for what it is. Your higher self and your higher truth can recognize real virtue over false. Through meditation and mindfulness practice you can pay attention to when the mind is being influenced by the self-serving ego. When you realize that your ego has caused you to miss the mark, acceptance creates the opportunity to begin again.

True Power

Acceptance opens the door to true power. By moving beyond the control of the ego, you submit to the path of virtue and wisdom through accumulating virtue. Wisdom is the accumulating and successfully implementing virtue to create a true destiny.

"...accumulating virtue means there is nothing one cannot overcome

when there is nothing one cannot overcome

one's limits are unknown

The limitations unknown, one can possess sovereignty

With this mother principle of power, one can be everlasting..."

Chapter 59, Verses 5 – 9, Tao Te Ching

Sovereignty, the mother principle of power, is only available if you choose to follow the path. Acceptance is the spiritual ability to seek and find the truth and clarity. Without this ability, the path leads to mistakes; ego created problems, unnecessary problems, and strife. So now that you know the true path to a successful destiny can you practice acceptance? Can you transcend the ego and take ownership of your life and destiny? The true path of sovereignty awaits you. Remember, with sovereignty, "the mother principle of power; there is nothing one cannot overcome." Be the Sovereign.

Acceptance

Acceptance

19

PATIENCE

"Thirty spokes join one hub
In its emptiness is the function of a vehicle..."
Chapter 11, Verses 1- 2, Tao Te Ching

Patience, as a virtue, is mostly seen indirectly in the Tao Te Ching. However, I believe it to be such an important concept virtue that it deserves focus.

Patience is what I would call a lynchpin virtue. It is the complement[36] to emptiness. Emptiness provides the space and opportunity for something to happen, for something to be. Patience provides the space and possibility for implimenting any virtue through choice. Being empty is to be in a mindful state; free of ego driven distracted feelings and thoughts. Patience is the ability to wait, then look and see what the best choice or action would be. In this instant, emptiness and patience are working together to provide this opportunity to pick, choose, and impliment any virtue. Those virtues are not able to be seen as a choice unless you are able to be still and be patient.

The Tao Te Ching uses a wagon wheel as a metaphor. The thirty spokes are like the different virtues that you can

---

[36] Complement; something that completes or brings to perfection (dictionary.com)

choose from. It represents the different perspectives, the different choices, and the different actions. Like the spokes, they are tied to one central place which is the hub. And the hub is empty, so the axle can turn (function). This is how the wagon is able to move forward smoothly.[37] Patience ties everything together. Without patience you can't impliment wisdom. You can pick any area of your life that you wish to improve with more discipline and better choices. You cannot begin to be successful until you can step back and be patient. Patience is not just some platitude or popular cliché. Patience is a very powerful enabler of wisdom. It is a prerequisite. It has to happen because your choices determine your destiny.

Patience creates the space for hope, giving you the courage to overcome fear. By the phrase 'creating space,' I mean that you become present and self-aware. Free of the impatient ego, you can choose to be patient. In the moment of patience, you return to your true path.

---

[37] See chapter 10, Emptiness, emptiness give function to form.

141

Continuing with the wagon wheel metaphor; let thirty spokes of the wheel be some of the many virtues one can practice as a sovereignty cultivator. Without patience, these virtues will probably not be chosen.

Exercise:

Here is a list of some important virtues that when mindfully practiced can transform your life dramatically and wonderfully. Some will be discussed in following chapters. Looking at the group of Tao virtues below, think about how well you practice them. Get a piece of paper and write each one down. Write down beside it a score from 1 to 5.

 1 is no patience and 5 is the patience of a Saint. You probably ought to begin with honesty and work your way down. Do you have the patience to stick with this exercise? Alternatively, are you already telling yourself you will come back later?

Honesty

Acceptance

Wisdom

Will Power

Contentment

Courage

Discipline

Cooperation

Detachment

Gratitude

Generosity

Simplicity

Flexibility

Softness

Honor

Modesty

Hope

Tranquility

Service

Tact

Wonder

Listening

Seeing

Moderation

Try these powerful steps of cultivation. The following chapters on virtues require you to exercise patience and practice. Here are some actions steps for cultivation.

1. **Mindfulness**. Take a course in meditation and mindfulness. (See THE DIXIE TAOIST VOLUME ONE). Learn to pay attention to being distracted and become self-aware.

2. **Keep a journal**. I have found that it helps to keep a journal of some sort. At the end of each day, make notes in your journal of what you experienced.

3. **Cultivate patience** for a couple of weeks before moving onto the list of other virtues to incorporate into your life. Patience empowers self-discipline. Try to spend 2 or 3 weeks on cultivating patience and use your journal to chart your progress.

4. **Cultivate A Life Path of Virtue**. Start with the virtue that you scored the lowest on and work your way up to your best. The following chapters are some that I find very important cultivate. Take each virtue and live with it for a week. At the beginning of each day take a moment to set the intention to follow the virtue. Work your journal. You do not have to become an expert at virtuous living. Even just a modest improvement will transform your life. Just do the best that you can. Remember, that your choices will initiate cause and effect (karma). The causation of virtue will result in true wisdom which will guide you

to true success. What you concentrate on, what you send out, will return bigger, deeper, and stronger. The more you invest in virtuous choices, the bigger the return of mystic virtue. This is the foundation for a long and successful life. This is the way of sovereignty. Begin with patience and self-honesty.

Wisdom

20

WISDOM

"The ultimate purpose of the Tao Te Ching is to provide us with wisdom and insights that we can apply to life. If we cannot do that then it doesn't matter how well we understand the passage. The true Tao must be lived." Derek Lin[38]

I define wisdom as the intelligence that consciously combines knowledge and experience for sound judgment. Many books and articles use the phrase "wisdom of the Tao." I take that to mean, intelligence gained through study and practice of Tao lessons in everyday life. However, it is important to note the distinction between knowing the wisdom and using the wisdom. Acquiring knowledge alone is not enough. To benefit from the real power of wisdom you must cultivate it and use in the moment to moment choosing that creates your destiny. The opposite of wisdom is ignorance and stupidity. A colloquial definition of stupidity or ignorance is to keep repeating the same destructive mistakes but expecting new and different results.

There are two main points I hope that you will gain from this study of wisdom. One is to cultivate wisdom, and the other is to choose to use it.

Cultivating Wisdom

I believe that there are two parts to cultivating wisdom.

---

[38] Tao Te Ching: Annotated and Explained, Derek Lin

They are experience and knowledge. Of the two, experience is the key ingredient and knowledge is a by-product. Society tends to promote the opposite of this path which is striving for knowledge with little regard for wisdom. The pursuit of knowledge is something the ego is fond of when the motivation is vanity, greed, or to manipulate.

The distinction is that learning and training to build knowledge is sound when it is intended as a foundation to build experience. Later, when you have practiced what you learned from real life experiences, your wisdom will be true. The wisdom of the Tao follows the same process. You are to study the Tao lessons and gain experience through use in everyday life. Over time, you become conditioned to be guided by what you have learned through the teachings and your experiences.

Wisdom is found in both failure and success. One teaches you what leads to failure and one teaches you what leads to success. Over time, your experiences become the true wisdom.

The other point to know is that the gained experience must be applied. Wisdom has no value if you do not listen to it and use it. This may sound mundane, but it happens every time your ego overrides your wisdom. It is the reason that smart people make stupid mistakes.

"Yesterday I was clever, so I wanted to change the world. Today I am wise, so I am changing myself."
Jalaluddin Rumi [39]

---

[39] Paraphrased from various translation. These may not be an completely accurate.

Learning the sovereign ability to rule over the ego is the purpose of this book. In that important moment of choice you can be aware of the many options available. The voice of the ego will often be the loudest. Sovereignty is accessing your wisdom-mind whose intelligence is learned from both knowledge and experience. At that moment, you can override the emotional ego and make a wise choice.

Again, meditation and mindfulness practice will provide the presence of mind and awareness to make a wise choice. Without this skill, your mind will be captivated by the ego influence and the emotions that go with it. Emotions, mood, and desire can be the cause of the obvious mistake.

Tao cultivators can remain calmly detached from these negative factors so that the wisdom-mind can prevail.

The inherent power of wisdom is the right action of intelligence. One of the complements of patience is wisdom. Patience can provide the space and opportunity for wisdom by controlling the reactive ego. Detachment can provide the opportunity for patience. You can see these virtues work together, in a tapestry, to create wisdom. You just must be present and self-aware.

Wisdom is one of the power virtues of sovereignty. Moreover, remember what Lao Tzu stated in Chapter 59, verses 5-9,

> "...*Accumulating virtues means that there is nothing one cannot overcome*
>
> *When there is nothing that one cannot overcome*
>
> *One's limits are unknown*
>
> *The limitations being unknown, one can possess sovereignty*
>
> *With this mother principle of power, one can be everlasting...*"

Simplicity

Simplicity

21

SIMPLICITY

End sagacity; abandon knowledge
The people benefit a hundred times
End benevolence; abandon righteousness
The people return to piety and charity
End cunning; discard profit
Bandits and thieves no longer exist
These three things are superficial and insufficient
Thus this teaching has its place;
Show plainness, hold simplicity
Reduce selfishness; decrease desires.
Chapter 19, Tao Te Ching

If you look at a list of antonyms for virtue you will see words like dishonesty, evil, and, imperfection. Practicing these traits will end in ruin. All virtue has inherent power. You can see the inherent power in simplicity.[40]

The root of the word simplicity is simple. The term "simple" can be defined as: easy clear, uncluttered, and, natural.

Simplicity is a virtue because of its altruistic nature (selfless action). Those who are aware of the ego's desire for details and complexity know how it can hide cunning and trickery. If you look up the antonyms for simplicity you will see complexity, difficulty, and complication.

---

[40] See chapter 16, True Courage, subsection Inherent Power

The complement to simplicity is honesty. Those who are honest with themselves and others feel no need to make things anything other than easy, clear, straightforward or natural. Telling the truth keeps things simple. Lying is complicated because of the difficulty in keeping the details straight. The more the lie is defended, the more complex it becomes. Often it will evolve into something indefensible, and it will become painfully apparent that the truth would have been much simpler.

Another complement of simplicity would be conservation. The vanity of ego can be the source of non-useful expenditures of resources. Complexity leads to difficulty and complication, which ultimately leads to stress and worry. Stress and worry generate a need to cope which drains your energy and resources.

A good example of this can be seen with the late genius and entrepreneur Steve Jobs. It is said that he wore the simple attire of jeans and a black shirt as his primary wardrobe. Not having to worry about what he wore must have freed up his genius for more creative wonders.

Exercise/Example

Imagine what the simple life would be for those who are cultivating sovereignty. What if you lived a more simplistic life? Consider areas of your life and how simplicity would have a more positive effect on something like your financial picture.

- Are your finances complicated? Why?

- How much debt do you carry that is due to non-essential needs?
- Why did you choose:
  - the car you drive
  - The clothes you wear
  - The person you married
  - The house you bought
  - The church you attend
  - The person you voted for

Often, coping means buying stuff to make yourself feel better and bring you happiness. This coping can become a circularity for suffering. Because of problems, you might feel "if I could just get that _____(fill in the blank) I'd be happy." So you spend money and get one. One day you realize that you are still unhappy. Then you buy something else. At some point you may realize that you have acquired too much debt. You can now add debt and financial problems to your unhappiness. Searching for happiness in material possessions often creates a downward spiral.

The chain of complexity might go like this:

  - Complexity leads to a higher potential for problems to occur.
  - Problems create stress.
  - Stress leads to unhappiness.
  - Unhappiness leads to coping.
  - Coping leads to desire.
  - Desire creates attachment.
  - Attachment leads to striving.
  - Striving leads to complexity.

When you can learn to find true joy and happiness in the simple things, usually non-tangible items, you can find lasting joy and happiness.

This concept always hits the ego the wrong way. So, if you feel resistant to the idea of living a simple life, free of attachments, that is the ego influencing your mind and mood. Sovereignty is the ability to reign in the ego and find the power of simplicity.

This is where simplicity becomes a virtue of power.

- Clarity
    - Simplicity gives way to fewer problems.
    - With fewer problems, there will be less stress.
    - Less stress means less striving.
    - Less striving creates unattached action.
    - "With unattached action, there is nothing one cannot do."[41]

The phrase "*nothing one cannot do*" is a pretty good example of success. Simplicity is a virtue that can lead to success. Constancy, which is returning to self-awareness and unity with the Tao is easier when life is free of distractions of attachment.

If you are keeping a journal, notate the times where you are successful at keeping to simplicity. As you are cultivating sovereignty you will have setbacks. Remember that a

---

[41] Chapter 48, verse 5, Tao Te Ching.

setback is an opportunity to cultivate sovereignty and to get back on track. Be mindful of the choices that lead to complexity and see the ego's influence in your decision making.

Example: *Because she kept things simple and easy to understand, the project was completed smoothly and quickly.*

Practicing the virtue of Simplicity enables Sovereignty. Sovereignty is "the mother principle of power."[42]

---

[42] Chapter 59, Verse 9, Tao Te Ching

Simplicity

22

MODERATION

"...Therefore the sage:
Eliminates extremes
Eliminates excess
Eliminates arrogance..."
Chapter 29, Verses 12 – 15, Tao Te Ching

I define moderation as avoiding excess or extremes.
Complements of moderation are balance, harmony, and
conservation. There is inherent power in the ability to
moderate behavior and choices.

Understanding moderation is not rocket science.
Implementing moderation can be quite challenging. Any
reasonable person knows and understands that going to
the extreme in any situation erodes balance and well-being
and that excess leads to depletion. Most people know this.
Then why do so many people suffer from some form of
excessiveness or extremism?

In most cases, suffering is a result of the cause and effect from the choices made by the ego. When one ego becomes excessive and receives notoriety then other egos will feel envious and begin to follow it. This behavior will begin with one person and often spread to include many other people. When the egos of many collude, it becomes collective ego. It is easy to observe how an individual or a group of people are out of balance. The result of extreme or excessive behavior is evident by the lack of harmony. Here are some examples of being out of balance or to have disharmony to consider:

- Health and fitness harmony (weight, vitality, energy)

- Mental and emotional peace (self-destructive behaviors and habits)

- Financial health (income and debt balance)

- Interpersonal relationships (how well we get along with others, cooperation, teamwork, friendships, familial relationships)

If you are experiencing an imbalance of any of these, try realizing where a lack of moderation has created disharmony. The deeper insight will be to realize how ego played a role in the choices that led to excess. You can use moderation as a conscious management of decisions and actions so that balance and harmony are maintained in all aspects of life. Moderate choices are only possible when you have learned to manage the ego. Management of the ego is the self-discipline of sovereignty.[43]

THE INHERENT POWER OF MODERATION

We all have experienced challenges in life. Things happen to us, and we find ourselves in stressful situations. When they do the ego is quick to react often overreacting. These are the times when we are most likely to go to excess or extreme. The Sovereign is mindful of ego reactions and chooses to use a moderated response.

Here is an example where you can see the inherent power of moderation.

> Because of her moderate approach to gambling, in Las Vegas, she was able to leave the casino with her winnings and invest them in real estate.

> The lesson: because she managed the ego's lust and greed for more she wisely left while she was ahead. She was then able to invest the net gain winnings into something with stable growth. This example involves other virtues as well as their inherent powers. In this one, you can see: patience, wisdom, moderation, conservation, and constancy.

---

[43] To gain control the ego, see the Chapter 5 on Meditation and Mindfulness.

> *"...Excessive vitality is said to be inauspicious*
>
> *Mind overusing energy is said to be aggressive*
>
> *Things become strong and then they grow old*
>
> *This is called contrary to the Tao*
>
> *That which is contrary to the Tao will soon perish..."*
>
> *Chapter 55, verses 14 – 18, Tao Te Ching*

I included verses from Chapter 55, because they are directly relevant to our modern life.

Excessive vitality

Too many people strive to be successful. People abuse their bodies while striving for success such as consuming too much caffeine or energy drinks due to fatigue and lack of sleep. This, along with staying up too late and partying all night is going against the virtue of conservation. Either way, the pursuit of extreme energy is known to create health problems.

Overusing Mind Energy

This term has many examples. However, the one that I want to focus on is worrying. Being concerned about potential problems is a regular part of life. Chronic worrying can quickly become toxic. Too much anxiety is stressful and causes a serious imbalance in the mind and body. Many self-induced sicknesses have their beginnings in worry-stress. Again the antidote for this is meditation and mindfulness.

Karma

Now is a good time to remind you of the relationship between moderation and karma.[44] Remember the relationship between choices and cause and effect. Your future; your destiny is being created in the present. When you act or react with extreme measures the future results will be even more extreme and problematic. Taoists call karma "the great executioner" because it does not play favorites and you cannot hide from it. No one is exempt. In this regard it is imperative to use moderation as a management tool to prevent a dreadful destiny. Moreover, your circumstance now can be understood by what you did in the past. Take another look at the list in the beginning of the chapter, of areas in your life that may be out of balance. These are the results of some choices or reactions from the past. They may be a result of your own decisions or from others. If they are from others, you must still be mindful of how you respond and use moderation as a guide. This insight is also a reminder of how your choices can affect other people. Moderation is the wise approach.

The Sovereign takes care in moderating each step along life's path. The Sovereign is aware of how choices affect themselves and others. The Sovereign is mindful of the fact that all things are connected, and creates a destiny that serves everyone in the best way by avoiding ego-indulgent

---

[44] See Chapter 10, Karma (under Tao principles)

choices. That is the power of moderation; conserving and preserving life by preventing extremism.

Moderation

Softness

23

SOFTNESS

The softest things of the world
Override the hardest things of the world
That which has no substance
Enters into that which has no openings
From this I know the benefits of unattached actions
The teaching without words
Are rarely matched in the world
Chapter 43, Tao Te Ching

Softness is both a Tao principle and virtue. In this book I am putting it under the category of a Tao virtue because of its inherent power. The first two verses reinforce the inherent power of using softness to overcome hardness. The most commonly used metaphor and easiest to understand is water. Water is soft to touch and has little substance when you try to pick it up. Stone is the commonly used metaphor for hardness and a material which has no apparent openings. To appreciate the inherent power of softness penetrating something hard, look at the Grand Canyon in the American Southwest. Water has slowly worn away the hard and rocky plateau to create one of the great wonders of the world. It is also quite evident when you look at a sandy beach or a sandbar. Water has reduced solid rock into tiny particles. The process begins with water slowly penetrating the hard surface of the stone. Slowly and patiently water seeps into the rock in a process that disintegrates its structure. Wind and sun, also without substance, assist the process until the solid stone is no longer there. The power of softness is especially useful in dealing with some of the personality traits of the ego. Some of those hard characteristics might be stubbornness, anger, and aggression. The soft approach to these would be patience, non-reaction, or empathy.

Nothing in the world is softer or weaker than water

Yet nothing is better at overcoming the hard and strong

This is because nothing can replace it

That the weak overcome the strong

And the soft overcomes the hard

Everybody in the world knows

But cannot put into practice

Therefore, the sage says:

The one who accepts the humiliation of the state Is called its Master

The one who accepts the misfortune

Becomes king of the world

The truth seems like the opposite

Chapter 78, Tao Te Ching

The hard and the strong can be problems or obstacles that seem impossible to overcome or solve. Yet the soft approach of virtue can overcome these too, just as water overcomes stone. Patience, acceptance, and flexibility are powerful virtues that can overcome hard problems and hard people.

Here is a story that I will share to reflect how softness can overcome hardness in interpersonal relationships.

In the city where I was living, there was a consignment shop that I affiliated with as a vendor. It was during the great recession. Times were hard, and people experienced much stress trying to make ends meet. The owner and manager of this consignment shop had a challenging time trying to keep her business going. Her stress created much tension among the people who worked there. Because of her anxiety, she was not a good manager, and retention was a problem. One of the more successful vendors, a lady who had experience in the antique market decide to leave and start her own business. She was a friendly and optimistic person who finally had enough of the stressful environment and opened up a similar business across the street. She was an immediate success. Most of the customers stop going to the business of the cranky lady and started giving business to the friendly lady. Then many of the customers, vendors and workers, having had enough of the constant drama, left and came over to the new business too. It did not take long before the first business was in serious trouble with a lack of loyal customers and workers. One day which had been particularly bad for her, she got angry and marched across the street to have it out with the woman who had left and started the successful business. She threw open the door, walked up to the new store owner and begin to bless her out. Momentarily, she paused in her onslaught to take a breath. During her verbal attack, the other woman, the friendly optimistic and prosperous new store owner smiled and said, "Oh honey, I am so sorry you are having such a hard time. I know how difficult it is. Let me hug you". She embraced the angry woman, who suddenly wilted and began to sob. She returned to her store, and before long it was closed and out of business. Later, she came to work at the new store for the friendly lady. The last time I saw them they were both at peace and happy again.

In this true story, the friendly optimistic lady used a soft, non-reactive, empathetic, and compassionate response to the hard attack. It is a classic case of wisdom vs. ego. Witnessing that event raised my spirit, and to this day, I keep that example in my mind as a strategy for dealing with hard personality types. I have told this story many times, and people have shared their own stories where they found it to be successful. In this chapter of the Tao Te Ching, wu wei activates the inherent power of softness.

"...From this, I know the benefits of unattached actions..."

verse 5[45]

---

[45] See the Chapter on Wu Wei; Section One

To see the inherent power, consider this sample sentence:

Because she reacted softly, with empathy and compassion, the woman stopped attacking her.

"...The teaching without words

Are rarely matched in the world..."

Chapter 43, verse 6-7

That woman taught me, and everyone there, how to use softness to overcome hardness for a beneficial outcome. We learned from her example. Later I asked her about it, and she said that she was living through her Christian conviction of *"love thy neighbor."*

It takes self-discipline of ego control to choose softness. Self-control and ego management is the greater principle of sovereignty. In the moment of action, you have a choice. If you are mindful of ego you can be detached from reacting.

To Overcome Hardness

Compassion includes empathy and caring. Pity will not inspire courage but love will. The caring of another being or cause become compassion when you move beyond the indifference of the ego.

With sovereignty, you can overcome the self-serving ego and allow compassion to rise above indifference. You cannot truly cultivate sovereignty without it. Practice and improve mindfulness skill so that you can find true courage. Be the Sovereign.

Softness

Flexibility

24

FLEXIBILITY

While alive, the body is soft and pliant
When dead, it is hard and rigid
All living things, grass and trees,
While alive are soft and supple
When dead, become dry and brittle
Thus that which is hard and stiff
is the follower of death
That which is soft and yielding is the follower of life
Therefore , an inflexible army will not win
A strong tree will be cut down
The big and forceful occupy a lowly position
While the soft and pliant occupy a higher place
Chapter 76, Tao Te Ching

The application of flexibility and its inherent power can be seen in these examples:

By virtue of its flexibility, the old willow tree was able to bend and snap back without breaking. The old pine tree was too stiff and snapped in two.

He received a lot more work requests because he was so flexible with his schedule.

The inherent power is endurance, sustainability, and longevity. When you are flexible, the negative emotional restraints of the ego do not bind you. The ego gets caught up in all sorts of tricky traps. It worries about how it looks. It will cling to its attachments and follow desire. This mindset is very rigid about acceptance. It will refuse to do the right thing with stubbornness.

With detachment, the spirit, free of the ego illusion, can be rational and realize success through compromise and negotiation. The ego is attached to specific outcomes and will stubbornly refuse to be flexible. The ignorance of the ego will be clueless about what the wisdom mind knows. It will stubbornly and blindly stumble its way towards the reward it has become fixated on. Often there is a relentless expectation of material gain that drives it. Being flexible is a mindful choice. You must be in a state of wu wei (unattached action) to follow the Tao.

That is self-discipline as the ruler of your inner kingdom; as the sovereign. Sovereignty is keeping the ego-animal mind in check so that you can make the smart choice.

Flexibility gives you the ability to be nimble on your imaginative feet so that you can successfully negotiate the challenges in life. It is why smart people do dumb things. When the spirit knows the wise action but the ego pulls the trigger, the odds of failure suddenly increase. The ego will check out reality and be under an illusion about how it feels life should be. By becoming detached from this outcome, you can take back control. Awake and aware, you can steer yourself back on course, which is the Tao (The Way).

In nature, flexibility is a survival strategy. Consider the Octopus. They have evolved and survived for millions of years due to their extreme flexibility. They can fit into the most unlikely of places to escape or hunt prey. In their natural way, they have unified with the Tao and have endured.

There is a direct link between your ability to control the ego mind and your skill at being flexible in reacting to life's situations. Being flexible reduces stress, tension and improves endurance. Controlling the ego and being flexible takes practice. However, it is an important skill that will enable you to survive and continue until the next challenge.

This ability, to manage the ego and be flexible is a powerful virtue of the Sovereign. Be the Sovereign.

Flexibility

Harmony

25

HARMONY

"...Knowing harmony is said to be constancy
Knowing constancy is said to be clarity..."
Chapter 55, Verses 12 &13, Tao Te Ching

Harmony is dynamic. It incorporates the Tao as a principle and a virtue.

Humanity's recognition of the Tao predates written history. There are some historians who believe it began as early as the stone age.[46] Early humans observed patterns in nature. In the sky, they saw constellations. They noticed weather patterns and climate in the natural world. Somewhere along the way they saw another phenomenon that we now call harmony. When you look up the definition of harmony online, you will see it defined as a "consistent, orderly or pleasing arrangement of parts." It also describes harmony as "congruent." Tao cultivators have a deeper realization and appreciation for harmony.

The chapter about Yin-Yang describes the nature of the Tao to be one that is always in a state of change between the two different polarities. The ancients observed these potential differences and called them Yin and Yang. They

---

[46] Eva Wong; Taoism; Shambala Publications 1997 et al.

realized that there are two points where the two approach and reach a temporary state of equilibrium. This approach towards each other is called convergence.

Convergence

The result of this karmic convergence is something extraordinary. Tao virtues are both opposing yet complementary to each other. You can realize this phenomenon by observing two bodies of water. They are both under the influence of gravity and hold the potential for movement. When water is restricted it cannot move. Yet when released, gravity will pull water toward a lower place of less water. Convergence is the coming together of the two bodies of water to a state of equilibrium.

Congruence

As the level of water in body reaches a level complementary with each other they become congruent. This congruent state is also known as harmony. As stated above, harmony is defined as an orderly and consistent arrangement of parts.

Most reasonable people will agree that harmony is a good thing. Harmony is many times equated with happiness, joy, well-being, and peace. These are all correct, yet you can realize an even deeper understanding. Many people desire harmony but are unable to find it or don't know how to create it. Most importantly, people become too distracted and forget what it is like to live in harmony. For the Tao cultivator, the "The Way of Virtue" is the means of cultivating the Tao of harmony.

Synergy

The word synergy is a modern word that describes the phenomenon that takes place when the interaction of many elements come together and the combined result is greater than the sum of their individual effects. The joining creates something special that is much more than what each part would ordinarily produce alone. This synergy is a Tao effect that you can observe in all aspects of nature, the cosmos, as well as the ethereal realm. Following a single Tao virtue can produce positive results in your life. Following the Tao (the way of virtue) will bring clarity.

Constancy and Clarity

Clarity is seeing things as they are. In a practical everyday sense this means to see the reality of your life without the distraction of the ego. To choose wisely, to follow virtue, you must be able to be the silent witness.[47] When your attention is captivated by ego (the voice in your head) then desire and emotion will dominate your mind and your choices. Cultivators who have cultivated constancy are

---

[47] See "meditation and mindfulness" in Chapter 4. The silent witness is the higher self which has transcended from ego.

constantly mindful of the ego tricks and learn how to stay detached. Through mindfulness you can cultivate harmony.

Moderation and Balance

Once you achieve harmony you practice keeping the balance. Moderating your actions keeps you from the extremes that erode balance.

To Be at One with The Tao

Consistent harmony brings about a convergence with the Tao. It means that you are congruent with the flow of the Tao as "the way." And it means that you are in attunement with the source of all things. It is the synergistic harmony between your spiritual essence and your physical presence. Oneness with the Tao is a profound state of being and can have incredible results.

The Inherent Power of Harmony

To reveal the inherent power of harmony we just must use the 'because of' [48] example to see it.

Example: The founder of Taiji, Zhang Sanfeng, lived for 170 years because of the harmony he cultivated between heaven and earth.

Example: Qigong Master Li Qing Yuen lived for 256 years 'by virtue of' the harmony of the three treasures.

---

[48] See Chapter 6, Mystic Virtue for more information on inherent power.

So, as you can see, the virtue of harmony is powerful.

The last example that I would like to share shows the essence of harmony in one of the most beautiful ways. Moreover, considered to be one of our better examples of what is possible. This example is the convergence of nature, mind, body, and spirit.

Music - One of the definitions of harmony is the when the simultaneous combination of tones into chords is perceived in a pleasing way to the mind. Our ears hear thousands of different sounds every day. They have meaning, but they usually do not elevate to the point where we become captivated by the way they make us feel. Music is something very human and quite extraordinary.

Imagine a group of people gathers and each is given a musical instrument. None of the people have any training on how to play music. When you get them all to play their instruments at the same time, what you will perceive will be noise. It will be just a random assortment of tones and sounds that have no organized unity. However, when you put together a group of trained musicians who have played together for some time, something special happens to the sounds. Skill and talent become congruent with intention. The people and their sounds combine in a collaborative union whose sum is greater than the parts. The result is something often very wonderful, and it is called music.

Music is exceptional on many levels. It is a long-held way to harmonize with the Tao.

Using music as a metaphor; imagine what happens when a Tao cultivator brings the many skills of virtue into resonance with each other. This convergence of your spirit in harmony with your physical existence forms a unity with the Tao. Flowing with the Tao of joy is the music of the soul.

Cultivating harmony is the work of the Sovereign cultivator. Be the Sovereign.

Section Three

Cultivating the Self, First

Work On The Self, First

26

WORK ON THE SELF, FIRST

"YESTERDAY I WAS CLEVER, SO I WANTED TO CHANGE THE WORLD. TODAY I AM WISE, SO I AM CHANGING MYSELF" RUMI[49]

The Strategy: Always Work on your 'self' first, strategy and goals are secondary.

Before you can work on your strategies and goals you must lay the foundation for self-discipline. The first discipline that you must commit to is to cultivate your 'self' first. Cultivating the 'self' means to awaken as the true self and then control the ego-self. Self-awareness is the heart and soul of self-discipline. Only the true self can control the

---

[49] Paraphrased from various sources. While it may not be completely accurate, I feel that the concept is in alignment with Tao philosophy of working on the self, first (sovereignty).

188

ego-self.[50]Cultivating self-discipline is done in a state of self-awareness. Cultivating the true self is cultivating virtue and wisdom. So, before you start adopting strategies and goals you must have the wisdom to know which are in unity with the Tao. Without self-control, the ego will lead you astray by subjugating your strategies and goals. You will not be able to stay on the path without being mindful of what you are doing and why you are doing it. Once you commit to the cultivation of the true self, you can begin to have the clarity necessary for developing strategy and goals.

This uncommon insight was given to me early on by my Tao mentor, and I have found it be the most important first strategy to cultivate. Goals without willpower and self-control are just good intentions. The chances of not finishing are much higher without them.

"The road to hell is paved with good intentions"[51]

A Proverb[OBJ][52]

---

[50] For more about True Self and Ego, see the glossary in the back of the book on 'Self'.

[52] Internet sources seem to agree that this proverb originated with Saint Bernard of Clairvaux, C.1150, although the person credited with the most current adaption is James Boswell.

Work On The Self, First

The ego is blinded by its self-serving intentions. These so called good intentions of the ego will use virtue as the means to an end. Self-awareness is an important skill that will help with paying attention to ego-intent.

Ego-goals are well intended but almost always fail. Every January many people state a new resolution to accomplish a personal goal. Weight loss is a very common one, and we all know that the failure rate is very high. We lose our momentum towards the weight loss goal when we:

- cheat
- lose the will to continue
- become distracted (forget or don't pay attention to what we are doing)
- lie to ourselves
- set the goal for the wrong reasons
- lose our battle with desire

Only if you are mindful of your emotions, feelings, choices, and actions can you wisely navigate life to accomplish long-term goals. Goal achievement lies somewhere in the future. The steps you take to reach that point in your destiny are made right here and right now. That moment of choice is the point whether you remain true to yourself or fail at self-discipline. You must have virtuous clarity in picking your strategies and goals otherwise you will be serving the ego's path of desire.

How to 'work on the self' begins with Meditation and Mindfulness.

27

CULTIVATING MEDITATION AND MINDFULNESS

"...In holding the soul and embracing oneness
Can one be steadfast without straying? "
Chapter 10, Verses 1 & 2, Tao Te Ching

The Practice: Learn meditation and mindfulness so that you can transcend the ego-self. [53]Make your meditation and mindfulness practice a routine of discipline whether you want to or not. Be aware that it is the ego that abhors stillness and non-action.

How to work on the self

I have had many conversations with people about how to cultivate self-discipline. Self-discipline is exercised in a moment of choice. Lack of self-discipline is the ego always following the desire of the moment. A loss of discipline sometimes happens when raw emotion overwhelms us. Fear and anger can drive us to take self-destructive actions. In the critical moment of choice, you will be faced with whether you will give in to it or not.

Meditation is a state of being, and a higher state of consciousness. Being able to bring your focused attention above and beyond the crazy mindstream of thought and emotion is the most powerful skill that you can attain. It is

---

[53] See Chapter 5, Meditation and Mindfulness

also the hardest skill that you will ever work on cultivating. It takes practice. In the beginning, meditation practice is the most difficult. It can also be very difficult during times of striving and suffering. Ironically the times we need stillness the most is when the ego will reject it the hardest. If you are new to meditation, you must remember that you have been conditioned all of your life for undisciplined mind-wandering. Focus and concentration are skills that you cultivate through practice.

Find an instructor who can teach you the basics. It should not be a complicated technique. In the beginning, learn some type of mindfulness meditation. This will be your foundation. Make your practice a discipline. In the beginning you will look forward to your practice when the experience is still new. But there will come a time when you find that you just don't want to do it. It is important to recognize that this is happening and the source of the resistance. This source of stopping or giving up is the ego.

Once you have gained the skill to manage mind-wandering you can try other forms of meditation such as contemplative or self-reflection meditation. The techniques are not what is hard, it is the discipline to practice correctly and consistently that is the most difficult.

If you practice enough there will come a time when your skill matures into a relaxed transition into the stillness. You will know when this happens because you will be free from the pull of ego and mind-wandering. You become the silent witness. This is becoming consciously aware without actively thinking about it. This is the center of being. The more you can experience this state, the more you become a part of this nature.

The more stimulated your mind is, the harder it will be to

relax. The ego will resist. It wants to be doing something all the time. The ego gets antsy and bored quickly. The more agitated or over-stimulated you are the harder it will be to sit in stillness. Try short periods in the beginning, then work your way up to longer sessions.

If you are extremely agitated from too much drama, or over-stimulated, you may find it impossible to sit still. If you just cannot sit there, don't give up, reschedule for a later time. Whatever you do, do not quit the practice. Eventually, the intensity of your anxiety will wind down, and you will be able to sit.

Over-stimulation effects sleep quality. Continued mental stress directly affects physical health. Most people are unconsciously seeking escape from their minds through various kinds of distraction. Stress is cumulative. Therefore, you must give it space and time to relax. When you learn to focus your attention on a single point, the chaos of the mind will begin to dissipate. When you return your focus to the object of anxiety it begins to gain strength again. The ego feeds on attention, so focus your attention on your breath or mantra until the mind becomes still. This takes practice but will be the most powerful skill that you can attain. The time spent will the most important investment you will ever make.

Constantly watching the clock is a distraction. Get a meditation timer or phone app to help you start and finish without having to wonder how long it has been. Constantly watching the time during meditation is the ego asking, "are we done yet?"

Don't judge it as good or bad, just sit. When you can rise above the crazy desires and emotions of ego, then you are able to take control of choice. Then you can choose the

195

right action. Right action is rooted in wisdom and virtue.

Mindfulness is being able to pay attention to mind and mood in a state of detached observation. With mindfulness you will see the ego-self rising but not let it do the choosing. So even though you may have all sorts of desires and passions, you will choose the right way. That is self-discipline. Like meditation, there are ways to help develop mindfulness during a busy day. There are phone apps that will periodically chime to help you wake up and be present.

You can come up with a whole list of wise life strategies, but *if you cannot break the control of ego, you will fail*. It is the reason smart people do some very stupid things. Wise strategies must be rooted in the true self. This is your spiritual identity as a living being, so it is through this state of being that you cultivate your life strategies and live by them with discipline.

Summary: Practice meditation and mindfulness so that you can be self-disciplined. The ego is a part of you, but it must be managed. Self-discipline is Sovereignty.

28

MANAGING DISTRACTION

"...Can one be steadfast without straying..."
Chapter 10, Verse 2; Tao Te Ching

The Practice: Cultivate a strategy for waking up and paying attention to what you are doing and why.

In the beginning, I had a hard time learning to be mindful during my active daytime activities. One day I had an idea when a co-worker got into trouble for always oversleeping and being late for work. We were brainstorming ways to deal with the problem and it occurred to me that mindfulness was sort of like that, only during your waking hours. The similarity being that distraction is not being present and aware like being asleep. So I came up with the idea to set my watch alarm to beep every hour so that I would wake up and return to being present. It turned out to be a transforming idea. In the first few months, I would always be so busy and caught up in whatever the drama of the moment was that I was surprised and even annoyed when the watch alarm would go off. However, then I begin to notice and pay attention to what state of mind I was in and to back away from it by following my breath for a few seconds. One day I noticed that I was automatically become present a moment before each hourly alarm went off. Even before the alarm would go off, I would find my breath and become present. I use the term "wake up" for becoming present.

I had become conditioned to wake up every hour. This practice began to make a big difference in my behavior and stress level. At least once an hour, I would wake up and realize what I was doing and make smarter choices. Often that choice was one to relax and de-stress. Soon I was even able to wake up and think about what I had been doing and if it was in line with my personal goals.

Then I set my watch to beep every thirty minutes. Moreover, like before, I soon became conditioned to become present just before the alarm beeped. My performance as a boss and leader improved dramatically. In every one of those awake moments, I could choose to listen and pick a wise and virtuous response. I learned to be empathetic, inspired, cheerful, insightful, and understanding. Our team began to perform well, and things ran a lot smoother. I began to enjoy my job. There were still problems and obstacles, but my newfound powers allowed me to work through them effectively. I also learned to create fewer problems by making smarter choices.

The power I gained came from learning to wake up and pay attention to what the ego-self was doing. Then awake, aware, and in charge, I made much more effective choices regardless of what the ego was freaking out about or needing.

Distraction

Distraction is the state of not being present. It is a part of life, but it must be managed and moderated. It becomes a problem when we get so caught up in the drama of the moment that we are unaware that we have slipped back over into the ego-self. Have you ever looked back on a dumb thing you did and realized that you knew better but just lost control? Have you ever said something in a

200

moment of passion that you deeply regret? When you look back on it, you will realize that you were just angry or frustrated. Even though it is understandable, it is not right.

Imagine being able to see what you are about to do or say and then step back from it and choose to do or say something else. Even though you are experiencing this storm of emotions you do not have to give in to them. That is the power of the transcended self.

At some point, I realized that I did not need my watch alarm to wake up anymore. In fact, I stopped wearing a watch all together. With lots of practice, you too can learn to be conditioned to be mindful of your thoughts and feelings. By staying ahead of these thoughts and emotions, you can step back from a bad choice and realize that there are other choices available.

Summary: Develop a strategy for training yourself to wake up and pay attention. Meditation is waking up as your higher being, and mindfulness is paying attention and being present to avoid bad choices. Real progress on mindfulness is made through experience. Experience is gained when virtue is applied in the moment of choice (action).

29

CULTIVATING MYSTIC VIRTUE

"...Mystic Virtue is so profound, so far-reaching
It goes opposite to material things
Then it reaches great congruence..."[54]
Chapter 65, Verses 13-15, Tao Te Ching

The Practice: Begin building a foundation for your virtuous path by studying and practicing mystic virtue. As a foundation for clarity, it will be "far-reaching."[55]

Once you have attained enough skill to be mindful of choice, you will then contemplate what to choose (right action). I am suggesting that your strategy should be that of building a foundation of action through mystic virtue. There will be a moment when you are consciously aware of a choice you are about to make. This moment is the threshold where you can implement virtue.

Why should your first consideration be mystic virtue? The

---

[54] Congruence is defined as an agreement, coming together into harmony. See Chapter 25 "Harmony".

[55] "far reaching" is defined as "having a wide range of influence" and "likely to affect many things at many levels".

answer is because of the dynamic nature of mystic virtue. If you read the chapter devoted to mystic virtue you will see two main elements bring about power. The first asks you to be mindful of the "two standards," and the second element of consciously choosing virtue activates the *inherent power*.
56

I define the two standards as being the choice between altruism and the ego. In that moment of choice you consciously choose to be aware of ego and what it is striving for, yet you choose to remain detached and align with virtue. This virtuous choice, actualized by karma, will create a much better result. This can be so profound that others around you will be surprised and think it mysterious. Remember from Chapter 7; you can use the phrase "because of" to define the positive result that comes from knowing the two standards and picking the spiritual solution over ego.

Example: Because of her choice to be empathetic, she won the election in a landslide victory.

The two choices (standards) were to either be empathetic or self-serving (politically correct). The inherent power is revealed *because of* empathy which resulted in a solid victory. This example could also be phrased as.

By virtue of her empathy, she won the election in a landslide victory.

So, your action step here is to be mindful of the two standards, find and choose the altruistic choice (not ego-self-serving). It can be joined with another virtue such as the one above; empathy.

---

56 See Chapter 7, Mystic Virtue.

Being mindful of both standards is important. You should be fully aware of both and understand how the tricky ego can subjugate the moral intention of empathy. Virtue is to be genuinely empathetic and compassionate for those who suffer. Ego will pretend empathy and care just to get the vote. This is an important distinction. You must know the tricks of the ego yet hold to true virtue.

When you practice this enough, it will become second nature to recognize the two standards. You will not only see it in your ego but also in others.

Summary: Develop your ability to be consciously aware of choice and the two standards at work. Choose the way of virtue.

Respecting Karma

30

RESPECTING KARMA

"...There exists a master executioner that kills..."
Chapter 74, Verse 7, Tao Te Ching

The Cultivation: Be careful and pay close attention to what you say and do because karma is going to expand it and bring it back to you.

As discussed in Chapter 6, the seeds of your destiny are planted with every choice. The bearing of this fruit is karma. The Tao does not play favorites, so karma is a law of nature that will affect everyone. If the ego-self makes your choices the chances for future problems are very high. When you follow virtue good fortune will be your reward.

Let's keep this simple. You are going to get payback for your actions and words. It is imperative that you seriously cultivate the ability to pay attention to the future that you are creating in the present. No one knows when the payback will return, but it is guaranteed that it will come. It may be in the next minute, or it may be in the next lifetime.

Mindfulness is necessary for making wise choices. The Sovereign cultivates mindfulness. You must be able to pay attention, with detached observation, to what you are feeling and what is on your mind. You must rise above petty ego distractions and think about your actions. If you are living your life in distraction the chances are that you are just reacting to everything that happens to you without regard to the consequences. Be aware of the moods and behaviors that you are experiencing and learn to rise above them to be virtuous.

31

CULTIVATING WU WEI

The softest things of the world
Overcome the hardest things of the world
That which has no substance
Enters into that which has no openings
From this I know the benefits of unattached actions
The teaching without words
The benefits of actions without attachment
Are rarely matched in the world
Chapter 43, Tao Te Ching

The Practice: Cultivate the ability to accomplish more by doing less (effortless achievement) and without striving. This is accomplished through detachment from the outcome. Be mindful of ego attachments and intentions initiate the reaction. Instead, choose right action through virtue in the Tao.

Wu Wei is a state of being. Remember in previous chapters that the meditative state is one of detachment and transcendence. In this state you rise above the ego to become the silent observer. Free of ego attachments, you can align your actions with the flow of the Tao. The flow of the Tao is life and nature unfolding moment by moment. As the true self (the transcended self) you have clarity and accept things as they are. Virtuous actions are *promulgated* through karma so that you accomplish more without striving.[57] The metaphor that my mentor used was to think of a surfer riding the wave. When the surfer paddles out against the surf he is striving. When he turns around and paddles *with* a big wave he is lifted and carried forward with effortless energy. All he must do is keep that harmony of balance between him, his board, and the wave.

The opposite of this is to be blinded by the ignorance of ego and to go against the nature of reality. The ego is attached to its desire seeking or emotional coping agenda. It cannot give up the pursuit even if it causes self-destruction. The ego is stubborn, short-sighted, and needy. It always confuses what it wants with what it needs. The sensation and experience are one of struggle, pain, and suffering to achieve the goal or get what it wants. Most importantly, the ego is never satisfied for long. So even if it gets what it strived for, it will soon be bored and begins a new quest. Day after day, year after year, a person gets worn down with the struggle and ensuing stress. Have you ever known someone who is not happy unless they are fighting and struggling with something?

In verse 1 and 2 of chapter 43 it specifically states that, "*the softest things of the world overcome the hardest things in the world.*"

Think of stubbornness or a rigid perspective as hardness. Think of acceptance and detachment from outcome to be softness. By being open-minded, you can gain many different insights that will inspire you to accomplish more by doing less.

---

[57] Striving is defined as struggling, fighting, and giving unnecessary effort, going against the flow etc.

Cultivation

The way to cultivate wu wei is through the practice of meditation and mindfulness. As the true self emerges it lets go of the struggle and accepts the way of virtue.

Example: One way to look at struggle versus going with the flow is to think about how to survive a rip current. Each year people drown trying to escape the rip currents that develop along the shoreline. They drown when they panic and struggle to swim against the current, become tired and are overcome.

Here are the instructions I observed on the internet:

- *Pay attention and be aware if a rip current is present.*

- *Get out of the water if you feel a rip current and the water is shallow enough.*

- *Remain calm, do not panic.*

- *Call for help if you are having trouble.*

- *Keep swimming parallel to shore until you are free from the pull of the current.*

- *Swim diagonally toward the shore when the current begins to subside.*

- *Pay attention to your energy (tiredness) and relax and float when you need to.*

Now think of a problem you are experiencing. See if you can apply the current metaphor to real-life situations.

- Pay attention and notice when things begin to become problematic. Don't let the ego over-react or procrastinate. Practice proximity awareness. Avoid excessive distraction (be mindful of riptides in your life as they develop).

- Step back from the rip current if you can. Take a deep breath. Get out of the water when you first sense a rip current. A metaphor for avoiding situations that will lead to problems.

- Stay calm, don't panic. Be mindful of strong emotions influencing your perspective. Remain calm and do not panic.

- Seek guidance and wisdom. Seek clarity about the situation (call for help).

- Seek a way to turn the problem into an advantage; (lemons into lemonade. Swim diagonally toward the shore when you no longer feel the pull of the current.

Goals

When it comes to goals, wu wei is the best course of action. Cultivating wu wei is working on the 'self' first. Rather than a problem, think of the goal as the destination in life that you seek to arrive at.

Is the goal one that is in unity with the Tao (virtue) lessons?

Alternatively, is this goal just another ego-driven hunger?

Who benefits from this goal? Who suffers or gets exploited by the pursuit of this goal?

Here is the litmus test for personal achievement:

"No matter what it is you do, there is a way to do it that is effective, and enjoyable at every level. This is

the true meaning of Wu Wei"

Derek Lin, The Tao of Happiness

Wu Wei (detached action) takes cultivation and practice. Many times, in hindsight, you will see how you could have succeeded through unattached action. That is how wisdom and skill are developed through trial and error in real life.

Without the ability to be your true self and sovereign over the ego you will be a prisoner to attachments. These attachments cause striving. Attachment to the outcome is something you must be able to choose to let go.

Practice meditation and mindfulness as a discipline so that you can be present and aware of the rip currents occurring in your life. Be willing to see different perspectives, and you will be able to see how to "catch the wave" of effective, effortless, and enjoyable outcomes.

32

CULTIVATING PERSPECTIVE

The sages have no constant mind
They take the mind of the people as their mind
Those that are good, I am good to them
Those who are not good, I am also good to them
Those who do not believe, I believe them
Thus the virtue of belief
The sages live in the world
They cautiously merge their mind for the world
The people all pay attention with their ears and eyes
The sages care for them as children
Chapter 49, Tao Te Ching

The Practice: Practice being able to see things from different perspectives. The virtues of empathy and compassion become available when you can see from the perspective of others. Try not to be inflexible in your views. Realize that the wisdom lies within the ability to understand the many sides to the situations that arise.

In Chapter 8, you can see this diagram:

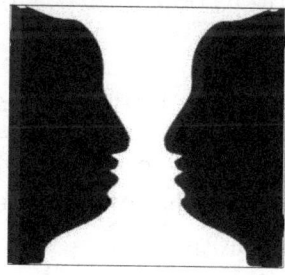

What do you see?

217

If you see a vase, you are correct. If you see the silhouettes of two people facing each other, you are correct. Which one do you see? Can you see the other? Try hard. This is similar to when you try to see a situation from a different perspective. Often there is an obvious one. Moreover, usually, there is at least one more if you look carefully.

You can use empathy when dealing with people. Just imagine what they must feel. Alternatively, you can contemplate how and why they see things as they do. When you realize the other perspective, you will suddenly have clarity. Clarity is seeing things as they are. If you only have one perspective, you do not fully have clarity, and your action or choices can miss the mark and cause even further problems. Spiritual Clarity is seeing the reality of something or someone with virtuous insight. You can use non-judgment, compassion, empathy, patience and others when you can see clearly both sides of situations.

To gain perspective and clarity, you must be sovereign over the ego-mind. The ego suffers from a lot of ignorant perspectives. It will have the perspective of:

- Greed, Lust, Desire

- Anger, Frustration, Revenge

- Vanity, Needing to be Right, Trying to Get Ahead In the World (greed)

- Trickery, Complexity, Intentional Ambiguity

Ego will be rigid in perspective, often only seeing its perspective or the perspective of its collective ego which is often organized as ideology.

As discussed in the last chapter, you can overcome the hardness of ego by implementing the softness of virtue such as

- Compassion

- Humility

- Patience

- Empathy

- Generosity

The way you cultivate and practice being able to see the different perspectives is, as always, found in detachment and mindfulness. Transcend the ego perspective (listed above) and gain clarity. Use the virtue of softness to overcome the hardness of the ego-perspective.

"Darkness cannot drive out darkness, only light can do that. Hate cannot drive out hate, only love can do that."

Martin Luther King Jr., Strength to Love, 1963

Summary: Seek different ways of seeing life, especially the perspective of others. Work towards gaining clarity and let Tao virtue and wisdom be your guide. Karma will handle the rest.

Cultivate Perspective

33

BECOME STILLNESS

The Tao is constant in nonaction
Yet there is nothing it does not do
If the sovereign can hold on to this
All things shall transform themselves
Transformed, yet wishing to achieve
I shall restrain them with the simplicity of the nameless
The simplicity of the nameless
They shall be without desire
Without desire, using stillness
The world shall steady itself
Chapter 37, Tao Te Ching

The Practice/Cultivation: Practice meditation. With practice, you will find stillness. Stillness is being and being is spirit. Spirit is sovereign and rules over the self (ego).

Stillness, emptiness, simplicity, humility, and softness are principles of the Tao that restore balance and harmony. Stillness is unity with the Tao. The Tao is void but also the source. The Tao has no agenda, yet it creates everything effortlessly. Unity with the Tao happens most effectively in stillness. When the mind is tranquil and observant, it is still. Stillness is the gateway to Tao creativity.

Stillness makes detachment possible. The relevant definition of detachment by Merriam-Webster is to be" indifferent" to worldly concerns or freedom from bias or prejudice. Stillness is the state of being where you are

222

indifferent "worldly affairs" and "bias or prejudgment [of the ego-self].[58] Sovereignty requires that you be free of these ego biases so that you can align with the Tao.

Meditation is the practice of transcending the distracted state of the ego. The transcended state is the stillness of being and unity with the Tao. This is the state of being from which wu wei, unattached action, is cultivated. This is the state of being to which you cultivate in attaining mystic virtue (knowing the two states, and unity with the inherent power of virtue).

Summary: Stillness is the foundation of sovereignty. Practice meditation and mindfulness to return to the Tao and gaining spiritual clarity.

---

[58] See Chapter 10 of the Tao Te Ching; verse 5. Lao Tzu asks/recommends being "cleaned away from the worldly view". Worldly view = status quo, following the herd, jumping on the band wagon, being politically correct et.

34

CULTIVATING CONSTANCY AND CLARITY

Attain the ultimate emptiness
Hold on to the truest tranquility
The myriad things are all active
I therefore watch their return
Everything flourishes; each returns to its root
Returning to the root is called tranquility
Tranquility is called returning to one's nature
Returning to one's nature is called clarity
Not knowing constancy, one recklessly causes trouble
Knowing Constancy is acceptance
Acceptance is impartiality
Impartiality is sovereign
Sovereign is Heaven
Heaven is Tao
Tao is eternal
The self is not more, without danger.
Chapter 16, Tao Te Ching

Constancy is defined in chapter 17 (of this book) as returning faithfully to the tranquility of stillness. Charity is being at one with the Tao and seeing and accepting things as they are. The opposite of this is be distracted with ego-striving, dwelling in illusion and lying to yourself. This may be the single most common reason for self-created problems that we humans practice. The one thing that is worse than lying to others is lying to yourself. Dishonesty to your true self is a form of non-acceptance. The source of self-deception is, of course, the ego. Acceptance of reality as it is, is a function of sovereignty. Sovereignty is true power. Cultivating sovereignty involves the cultivation of clarity.

"...Attain the ultimate emptiness
Hold on to the truest tranquility..."

Constancy is returning to the path and living with Tao principles as a way of life. The sovereign journey is one of learning to transcend the ego and return to spirituality and virtue. Acceptance is recognition through spiritual clarity. Spiritual clarity is the true self that has transcended the ego state of mind. This is the practice of meditation. Train in meditation to withdraw your attention from mind-wandering and concentrate on being and presence. Within this sanctuary you find and hold tranquility. Other spiritual paths have names for this state of calm abiding and bliss such as Samadhi and Satori. Free of ego, you can begin to be at one with the reality of the present moment which enables acceptance.[59]

---

[59] See Chapter 18; Acceptance (Section Two – A Study of Virtue)

The application of acceptance is in essence self-honesty. Chapter 11, titled Wu Wei, describes the virtue of not having an attachment to outcome. Free of attachment to outcome, from within the stillness of being, the true self practices *unattached action*. The ego can often become fixated on fulfilling a desire. The opposite to this is the ego perspective of non-acceptance and not seeing things as they are. Avoiding reality is a form of self-deception which is lying to your "self." The ego would argue that reality is malleable and subjective. The Sovereign knows that lying to yourself can lead to disaster.

You can become so absorbed within the ego-mind that you can lose touch with the true self (wisdom mind). This failure of constancy (returning to tranquility/stillness) leads to being lost within the ego paradigm of life where truth has little value. This distracted way of life will sooner or later lead to problems and suffering. At some point, the suffering can become so great that you feel trapped in a self-created prison that seems to have no escape. I would have you know that these prisons are illusions.

Letting go of desire (ego hunger) may sound simple. The door is wide open, and you can walk out into the light at the moment you begin to return to your true self. However, until you can get control of your mind and what occupies your attention, you are stuck in the ego prison. The door is wide open but your desire, ego desire, will hold you back.

Escape from ego is an awakening. It is cultivated through meditation and mindfulness practice. Self-awareness is the higher state of consciousness that you awaken to and realizes the spiritual being that you truly are. Then, and only then, can you control the ego. This is sovereignty. As the awakened Sovereign you can know reality and have clarity. You can let go of desire and direct your steps toward true freedom. Self-aware and paying attention to what the ego is striving for you can accept reality and navigate wisely and safely.

Self-honesty is cultivated through constancy and clarity. Wake up and be at one with the Tao. Self-aware; accept reality as it is. Choose actions that are unattached to ego outcomes. Use the higher faculty of spirit (sovereignty); to see the doorway of your prison and walk out into the light.

35

WANT VS. NEED

"Do not glorify the achievers
So the people will not squabble
Do not treasure goods that are hard to obtain
So the people will not become thieves
Do not show the desired things
So their hearts will not be confused
Thus the governance of the sage:
Empties their hearts
Fills their bellies
Weakens their ambitions
Strengthens their bones"
Chapter 3, Verses 1-10, Tao Te Ching

The Cultivation: Work on yourself to understand the difference between what you want and what you need.

As your mindfulness skill improves you will notice desire as it rises. If you are in a state of distraction you may not notice that you are making choices and taking actions strictly for the fulfillment of desire. In chapter 14, there is a paragraph about the virtue of Conservation that addresses want vs. need. Cultivating the virtue of conservation involves understanding the difference between something you want and things that you need. When asking the question "do I need this," you cannot rely on the ego to give the appropriate answer. The correct response requires self-discipline and the wisdom of virtue to understand the truth.

> *"One great question underlies our experience, whether we think about it or not: what is the purpose of life? ... From the moment of birth every human being wants happiness and does not want suffering. Neither social conditioning nor education nor ideology affects this. From the very core of our being, we simply desire contentment... Therefore, it is important to discover what will bring about the greatest degree of happiness." Dalai Lama*

The root of desire is found in the pursuit of happiness. Down deep we crave contentment. The awakened self (spirit) has the wisdom to be content and happy as a state of being. Yet the ego strives for happiness and fulfillment in that which causes more suffering. The desire and wanting can become so strong that the connection to spirit is lost and want becomes the illusion of need. You think you want it because it will bring you happiness.

> *"All suffering is caused by ignorance. People inflict pain on others in the selfish pursuit of their own happiness or satisfaction" Dalai Lama*

When the ego cannot have what brings it happiness then it suffers. The true self understands the desire, and that happiness is not found in what you buy but in how you live your life. Giving in to the illusion of wanting goes against the virtue of conservation.[60]

Cultivation of being able to discern what you want versus what you need is practiced through the skill of mindfulness. If you really want to have a moment of truth look at where you spend your money. Track your spending for the last six months and highlight those areas that fail to meet the 'what you really need' criteria. If you can think back, try to understand the underlying intention for those "want to have" items. The question to ask is "why did I want this?" If you can be honest with yourself, you can see how you waste many resources in pursuit of that which cannot be found.

As you do this, use moderation and seek balance. Managing wants and needs is about balance. If you deprive yourself of all wants you will probably fail. Have fun but be aware of what you are doing and why. Try to avoid attachments to the things you do to have fun. Enjoy the moment and let it go.

Sovereignty is being able to keep the ego and its wants and needs under self-control. Practice your ability to pay attention to your mind as it strives to fulfill a false sense of need.

---

[60] See Chapter 14, Conservation, one of the three treasures.

Listening

36

LISTENING

I opened a fortune cookie the other day. The fortune inside said,

---

"YOU CAN HEAR A LOT JUST BY LISTENING"

The Cultivation: Cultivate the skill of being a good listener. Understand what is being said, and the consciousness that is communicating with you. Learn to manage ego-distraction so that you can keep your attention on listening.

A long time ago I heard a sermon about listening. The story goes that during his presidency, Franklin Roosevelt noted that few people were paying attention to what he said. To see how true it was, he decided to test his theory out during a White House gathering. As he greeted each person he would say, "I murdered my grandmother this morning." Not hearing what he said, most people just smiled, nodded, and gave a courteous response such as "how nice" and "good for you." Finally, he got a real response when the Bolivian Ambassador responded with, "Well she must have deserved it."

Listening Defined: Listening is to be present and to give one's

235

attention to perception.[61]

Communication Lets begin with the obvious. When we are talking we are not listening. Even when someone else is talking, we *may* not be listening. The ears may be hearing, but you may not be *listening*. On a deeper level, the listening is done with the mind, and hopefully, consciousness paying attention. You are looking at someone while they are telling you something they feel is hugely compelling, only your mind is buried deep within your mindstream.[62] When something wakes you up, and you pay attention outward, and you realize that you had not heard a word of what was said because your attention was somewhere "upstream."

Listening goes deeper than that. This chapter is about *cultivating the skill to pay attention to what you hear*. Alternatively, deeper yet, it is to pay attention to what you perceive.[63] It is not just sound waves in the form of another person's voice. It is "hearing" what the consciousness behind the words is conveying to you.

Intuition. Listening is a complement of intuition. Deep listening leads to intuition. When you listen, you perceive. What you perceive, you can observe. You can listen to what you hear. That is unless your attention is deeply in mind-streaming.

---

[61] This definition was a composite from several sources

[62] Mind stream, or mind streaming is an ancient spiritual concept defined as the "moment to moment continuum of mind. The focus of your consciousness is often deeply concentrated in thought. A type of ongoing distraction creating a loss of presence.

[63] To perceive is the ability to see, hear, or become aware of something through the senses. *Or a way of regarding, understanding, or interpreting something; a mental impression*

Being able to stay focused and to listen requires not thinking at the same time. Recall what was discussed in the chapter on emptiness about it having functionality. Emptiness gives function to listening. Being empty creates the opportunity to perceive. Contrary to how this may sound, this is the highest form of waking consciousness. Note the following words that are listed at the beginning of this chapter.

The function of the ear ends with hearing,

that of the mind, with symbols or ideas.

But the spirit is an emptiness ready to receive all things.

Excerpt from the Chuang Tzu Chapter 4

As I have mentioned many times in this and other books, the ability to wake up from mindstream and pay attention, hold focus is a spiritual ability cultivated through meditation. It is applied over and over in your waking life through continuously becoming present and paying attention.

How can someone practice compassion and empathy if they are not hearing and understanding what others are trying to communicate? The ego cares little for what the other is saying unless there is a benefit or profit involved.

Try this the next time you are in a conversation with someone. Be aware that you are listening. Notice when your attention wanders. When you realize that your focus drifted; you re-focus back to listening (perceive/to pay attention). Listening with focused attention is a skill. When you practice it with the same person enough they will tell you that you are a good listener. The people in your life will regard you more favorably. They will also notice if you miss a lot because your mind is busy while they are talking to you. They will notice and be appreciative when you paraphrase what you are listening to with understanding of what they are saying and feeling. *Listening is what people who care about each other.*

This focused attention is to be applied often, but in a balanced way. There is a kind of harmony that you must achieve when you observe/listen to what is being said and processing the meaning. Being a good listener is an art that can be cultivated. It begins with not putting yourself first. It is best if you approach this with moderation.

While you are reading this, notice how the "inner voice" will comment. Alternatively, notice how your mind will drift off when you perceive some interesting concept. Your eyes and mind will still be processing the material, yet the attention is off in mindstream. Then you wake up and must go back and re-read the previous sentence. Sometimes it can be so thought-provoking that you must reread a few times. Stop right here, right now, and contemplate the meaning of this.

Spirit to spirit. Hopefully, you just took a moment to notice and contemplate how you listen and process, and now you are back. You went from listening to distraction, and now you are back listening. Interestingly, the information in my mind right now is taking a quantum leap and traveling through time and being perceived by your consciousness in some future date and some other location. From my consciousness in my present moment to yours right now in your present moment. Each spirit and mind separated by time yet connected. Perhaps listening is a quantum event. This is the power of being present in the "now," and such is the power of listening.

Listening

The final point is this; when you are present and still (out of mindstream), you are in the Tao. This is the Tao connection. When you are listening, and at one with the Tao, you are in the highest state of being. Your potential (what you are capable of) becomes unlimited when unified with the Tao. It is easier said than done. You can transform your life with even the smallest connection. You connect every time you become still and listen. Listen with constancy.[64]

The Sovereign cultivates the ability to return to the Tao and to listen. With a bit of work, you can gain the ability to listen to your thoughts with a sense of detachment. Within your true nature is wisdom. Being able to remove your attention from ego mind-streaming and know your wisdom is a very effective skill. Work at it. Become a good listener.

.

---

[64] See the Chapter 17 in Section Two; on "constancy". - returning to one's true nature

Talking

37

TALKING

Those who know do not talk
Those who talk do not know
Close the mouth
Shut the doors
Blunt the sharpness
Unravel the knots
Dim the glare
Mix the dust
This is called Mystic Oneness
Chapter 56, Verses 1 -9; Tao Te Ching

The Cultivation

To be mindful of your choice of words.

The mouth is connected to the mind. It's how people communicate what is on the mind. When the mind is under the control of the ego it can be used for non-virtuous intentions. The ancients realized how often the mouth can quickly get one into trouble. This is because it is a portal for the ego. The mouth and speaking are how the ego interacts with the outside world. In self- awareness, there is an instant just before we speak where we can realize what is happening and exercise the choice to silence the ego before trouble begins. The following chapters point to areas where we have an opportunity to desist from creating problems caused by engaging the mouth with the ignorance of ego.

Following are just some of the ways that the ego-mouth can create unnecessary problems.

Non-Virtuous Use of the Mouth (words):

Gossip

"Gossip is the Devil's radio." George Harrison

When the ego is feeling insecure and experiencing low self-esteem it will seek to feel better by bringing judgment on someone else. Ego's feed on the drama of someone else's pain, so they will share judgment with others for a collective celebration of someone else's suffering. The individual ego joins with others to form a collective. This mindset goes against the way of virtue which calls on Tao cultivators to be compassionate, empathetic, and supportive. The mouth is the transmission device of the ego-mind. Enjoying the pain and suffering of others, for any reason, is not the way of the Tao. Remember that karma plays no favorites, and what you put out into the world will, at some point, come back to pay you dividends.

Truth as A Weapon

"True words are not beautiful

Beautiful words are not true"

Chapter 81, Verses 1 & 2, Tao Te Ching

The cunning and clever ego will sometimes use words of truth with the intention of defeating or hurting another. While it is important to be truthful with others the intention behind using truth is what matters. The ego, by nature, is not caring nor compassionate so it will use words of truth as damaging weapons. Truth can be very hurtful and can even destroy someone's well-being. Truth should never be used to hurt someone or to get ahead of them.

Using Sharp Words as A Weapon

"...Blunt the sharpness..." verse 5

Sometimes the mouth and words are used as weapons to harm another person's wellbeing. While the words may not be truthful, their sharpness "can cut to the bone." The ego will try to look powerful or raise its self-esteem by saying something hurtful. It may be feeling revenge, anger, jealousy, or greed. Whatever the motivating force is, it can send one of its word daggers straight into the spirit. People have taken their own lives because of hurtful words spoken to them in a vulnerable moment. This is not the way of virtue (The Tao).

Contention

> "...Those who are good do not debate
>
> Those who debate are not good..."
>
> Chapter 81, Verses 3 & 4, Tao Te Ching

There are several reasons why the ego will contend with another person. When its self-esteem is suffering, it will argue just to be hateful and disagreeable. Sometimes it may be due to unfulfilled desire and resentment. Debate, contention, and arguing are some of the highest forms of non-acceptance. Debate in itself is not always a bad thing, it depends on the intention of the people involved. Debating can be useful in sharing ideas and clarifying thoughts. However, the debate becomes contentious when the intentions are to satisfy the ego. As mentioned before, the ego has many negative traits that motivate it to contend.

When it comes to words, Lao Tzu tells us to:

> "...Close the mouth
> Shut the doors
> Blunt the sharpness
> Unravel the knots
> Dim the glare
> Mix the dust..."
> Verses 3-8

Summary Be mindful of what you are feeling and what you are about to say. Pay attention to the inner intentions of the ego and stop consider what you are about to say.

> "If you propose to speak, always ask yourself, is it

Talking

true, is it necessary, is it kind." ~Buddha

Talking

38

BE THE GUEST

"...In using the military, there is a saying
I dare not be the host, but prefer to be the guest
I dare not advance an inch, but prefer to withdraw a foot..."
Chapter 69, Verses 1 – 3, Tao Te Ching

The Cultivation: Gain the ability to avoid instigating hostilities, and refrain from leaping into a fight. It is better to be careful and give the aggressor a chance to indicate intentions and plans. Give yourself the opportunity to prepare. It is always possible the attacker will get tripped up and hang themselves. This means that there is a good chance that the over-reaching ego of the aggressor will bring about their misfortune and cause their downfall. Moreover, thus you may achieve victory by doing nothing.

In verse one, the term "military" can be taken literally or figuratively. In a physical skirmish try to wait and see what the attacker's intentions are. Look for an opportunity to gain the superior position. Figuratively, "military" is your defensive response, a non-physical assault such as words or gestures.

This strategy is to not initiate an attack. When one comes at you it is better to step back and evaluate. The metaphor of host and guest comes from the old ways of letting the host direct the activities that the guest will enjoy. The guest just sits back and follows the lead of the host.

In many life situations, it is better to sit back and see what happens. This buys time to get insight and clarity on what is happening before making choices and acting. This perspective takes mindfulness of your reaction and intent. With sovereignty, you can exercise patience to take a wait and see approach. This simple strategy is an example of wu-wei where unattached action achieves success; accomplishing more by doing less.

39

DEAL WITH PROBLEMS EARLY ON

"When it is peaceful, it is easy to maintain
When it shows no signs, it is easy to plan
When it is fragile, it is easy to break
When it is small it is easy to scatter
Act on it when it has not yet begun
Treat it when it is not yet chaotic"
Chapter 64, Verses 1-6, Tao Te Ching

The Cultivation. Learn to deal with obstacles, problems, and situations while they are small and manageable. Later they will become too large, cumbersome, complicated, or scattered to deal with.

250

In the last chapter, "Be the Guest," you were encouraged to step back and let the situation develop. The wisdom of this chapter is to deal with small problems or obstacles before they become too large or too entrenched. So, there is a balance between being too aggressively reactive to a situation and procrastinating until things are too difficult.

Unfortunately, I have much experience with what can happen when you put off and avoid dealing with situations and problems that appear on the radar. I know what it feels like to be so beat down by life that you just sometimes can't deal with stuff. Here is what I learned. You have a date with Karma whether you want to or not. Doing and not-doing both have a result. Sometimes not-doing can initiate a series of changes that will come back in the future and slam you hard. So, sometimes you have to just deal with them. The wisdom is to begin the process early on before it becomes too overwhelming

Example: Once someone close to me received their car tag renewal in the mail. It only cost $21 to renew and get the correct date stickers for the upcoming year. This person put it off and soon forgot to take care of it. Later she lost her job and did not have the money. so she put it off even longer. Then she could not pay her car insurance and the policy was canceled. When the insurance company canceled the policy they let both the bank and the state department that registers automobiles know that the insurance had lapsed. One day she was driving home from the new job she finally landed when the police pulled her over because of the expired tag. Then they arrested her for driving without insurance. Her car was impounded, so she had to walk or ride her bike 14 miles to work in the July heat, in the crazy Atlanta traffic. She went to court and managed to get just probation, but she was also given a stiff fine. She had to come up with a lot of money (about $1000), which she had to borrow. She also had to report to the probation office once *a week. All of this happened because she did not promptly deal with a $21 tag fee promptly.*

I have described wu wei as unattached action. Wu wei is acting without attachment to the outcome.[65] However, there comes a time for wise action. Life will hand you a situation where avoiding or delaying will create undesired consequences. Therefore, the wisdom is to handle these situations and problems before they become too large, too hard, too fragile, too complicated, too expensive, too late, or just too chaotic.

Recognize the feelings and reasons for avoiding and not wanting to engage the situation. Are you fearful or lazy? Be honest with yourself so you can find courage. Remember "true courage"[66] comes from compassion. Face the problem with courage and seek wise action that will enable you to endure with strength.

How do you cultivate this strategy?

- Cultivate your mindfulness skills and pay attention to your emotions.
- Cultivate your ability to know when to act.
- Cultivate your ability to deal with problems and obstacles while they are still easily manageable.

There is a balance between acting impulsively and procrastinating.

- Step back and pay attention to how the emotional mind is reacting (detached observation).

---

[65] 1See the Chapter 11; "Wu Wei" in section one of Tao Principles
[66] See Chapter 16 True Courage; Section Two; a Study of Virtue

- Consider the consequences for action or no-action (karma/cause and effect).
- Consult your own life experiences to know when and how to act (wisdom).

Allow compassion to give you the courage to deal with problems or situations while they are easy to manage.

The Wisdom of Simplicity

40

THE WISDOM OF SIMPLICITY

"Show plainness; hold simplicity"
Chapter 19, Verse 10, Tao Te Ching

The Cultivation. Learn to keep everything you do simple.

As always, ego intention can be found at the heart of self-created problems that happen out of ignorance. One of the common mistakes the ego makes is to create complexity and chaos through its self-absorbed traits like a contrivance, vanity, impatience, and overreaction.

With skill at being mindful, you will be able to resist these behaviors and follow a strategy to keep things unambiguous and simple. Too much complexity creates the potential for things to break down or go wrong.

The skill of sovereignty will help you manage the ego as it tries for excess so that it will not create unnecessary complications.

Remember the old saying:

> *K.I.S.S. "keep it simple stupid."*

The Wisdom of Simplicity

41

RAISING THE SPIRIT

The Cultivation. Learn the ability to raise the spirit and experience the Tao of joy. You can realize the simple joy of living even, or especially during, the inevitable times of difficulty.

Moods and low feelings of the ego can bring down spirit. Our spirit can be lost from our higher consciousness and captivated by the materialist ego. The joy of the Tao can be found through the returning to the unity with the Tao; transcending the ego identity and recognizing the spiritual being that you are.

Spirit in this sense is the sense of morale, self-well-being, or mood which can be affected by the emotionally reactive ego-mind. Ego reacts to things that don't go its way in life with a negative emotion. These negative emotions will often set the mood and define life at that moment. The alternative is to rise above this reaction and choose a different sense of self. To raise the spirit you must return to spirit. Spirit raises spirit.

258

"In holding the soul and embracing oneness

Can one be steadfast without straying?"

Chapter 10, Verse 1, Tao Te Ching

Constancy

One of the virtues of Tao cultivation is Constancy.[67] Constancy is returning to the Tao. Returning to presence is a return to spirit. This awakening is the essence of raising the spirit. This true self is what wakes up from the dream-state of ego and its materialistic desires. When desires go unfulfilled, the ego becomes depressed at the loss. When you allow your mind to become entrapped by the ego you experience life in a pure ego state which can often be one of suffering. Returning is the waking up from this low conscious state into a self-aware consciousness, at one with the Tao. When your spirit raises you rise above those feelings and mood. Meditation is the process of waking up and realizing who you are in the stillness between thoughts. What I am describing is not easy. It takes much practice through real-time events of your life experience. However, even just a little experience can change everything. Even a tiny moment of returning, of attaining the stillness of the Tao, can change the course of your life.

---

[67] See the chapter on Constancy in Section Two; Accumulating Virtues.

259

This is your sanctuary and home and the center of life.

Mood and Feelings

Mood is no small thing. Mood can act as a kind of distorted reflection giving negative meaning where there need not be one. Like rose colored glasses, moods can taint your outward view of the world. This filtered view effects decision-making and perspective which in turn affects choice. Choice creates destiny both in the near and far future. This mood can become a mindset which acts as a dark prison from which you choose not to escape. All you may see is doom and gloom. It can become habitual and over time will create a life of misery. In a weird sort of anti-joy, I can remember days when I was not happy unless I had things to feel bad about.

By meditating and being mindful you can return and become the detached observer. Be mindful and realize how it is the mood that is creating the dark world you are experiencing. In the moment you become present, as spirit, you can raise your spirit (morale) *if you choose to*. To raise your spirit, you must take charge over your ego and turn away from its whiny voice that wants to give up and embrace despair. You must set an intention to change your mood, and you must use willpower to get you there. If you want to feel better you will. Be patient because this can take effort and time. You must keep returning to presence and letting go.

Imagine being able to shift gears when you realize what is happening to you. Suddenly you wake up and see what you are doing or saying and realize the mistake. Then you can look for and find better moods and feelings to come to your mind. You empower this to happen by focusing on things that can help you feel better. This is spirit focusing the mind instead of ego controlling the focus. Your spiritual intention fills the mind with an essence that inspires and brings about better feelings. When you can sustain these feelings, the mood will shift.

Raising the spirit is not so much as making yourself happy as it is about transcending negative thought patterns. You may be just trying to survive something and need courage and positive energy to endure. Cultivating this skill is hard work. It takes practice.

What are some sources to fill your mind with positive feelings? Here are some examples to just get the pump primed. Ultimately you will find your own sources and methods for raising the spirit. Because the best ones come from being inspired, they are unique and personal. The main thing is to proceed through self-awareness and filter them through the Tao teachings.

Here are some examples of how you can raise your spirit and ascend the that dark place that can become your prison.

Archetypes

Countless books and movies tell the story of how a down-fallen character makes a come-back from failure. These feel-good stories all have one thing in common; to raise the characters spirit enabling them to rise above defeat or death. The details may vary, but the message is the same. Who is someone you have heard of, or know about, that inspires you? A close friend of mine uses Rocky Balboa to inspire her when she has been knocked down. Even the movie theme song can give her an inspiring lift. When you are feeling knocked down, melancholy, and hopeless, think of what your archetype would do. You might even have 2 or 3 archetypes for different scenarios. You can put up posters in your office or even place a photo on your smart-phone screen to help you remember to rise up from a setback. By having an archetype, you can capture the spirit of their story and become inspired.

Affirmations

Sometimes you will hear something that inspires you. You try to remember it so the next time your spirit is low you can revive yourself. Sometimes you will come up with your inspired affirmations after you have experienced something profound and want to keep it at the ready.

Here is one I remember while attending a course in confidence for public-speaking. Public speakers know that you can better inspire others when your spirit is strong.

> *"I am going to be a storm-a flame-*
> *I need to fight whole armies alone;*
> *I have ten hearts; I have a hundred arms;*
> *I feel too strong to war with mortals-*
> *BRING ME GIANTS!"*
> **Cyrano de Bergerac**

I found that affirmations work. Especially when you need to dig deep and find courage just before a difficult action you must take. A powerful affirmation can come from the wisdom of one of your archetypes. By virtue of the examples, these legends lived, and their words of wisdom can be articles of faith when you need to find strength and rise up.

Be mindful of the ego and its tricks. What I am talking about is not arrogance or glory seeking but rather the strength of faith, confidence from experience, and most importantly, courage from compassion. [68]

When facing a monumental task, you can become overwhelmed and lose confidence. Your spirit can drop, and you give up before having begun. One of my favorites is,

---

"A journey of thousand miles begins beneath the feet."

Chapter 64, Tao Te Ching

It reminds me to not get caught and overwhelmed by large objectives. This is the wisdom of breaking up large tasks into smaller ones. In doing so, you take necessary action in the present moment. Right here, right now, I just focus my mind on this step. When this is over, I just focus on the next step. My faith in this Tao process lets me relax. Relaxed my spirit rises, and harmony is present. I can endure and

---

[68] See the Chapter on the three treasures, specifically compassion. True compassion comes from courage.

continue onward one step at a time.

Activities

Singing

What is one of your favorite songs that has a spiritual message? Sometimes when my spirit is low I sing to myself. As horrible as it [my voice] sounds, it will raise my spirit and get my mojo back. The songs that I am thinking of are not necessarily religious, but spiritual in a virtuous sense. However, if religious songs or hymns raise your spirit, then sing away with all the heart and gusto that you can. Don't hold back and "let it rip."

Listening

Sometimes listening to music because of what it stands for can raise the spirit. The first example could be the Rocky theme song (mentioned above). Sometimes the lyrics can help you first to grieve, and then to move on. When it is time to move on, or to rise up, listen to something positive and inspiring. Alternatively, another perspective is to listen to soft music such as spa music or easy listening. Relaxation is inspiring because the Qi will come up as the tension goes down. Sometimes I play music in Tai Chi classes. The intention is to raise the spirit which will then raise the Qi softly. You quite literally feel beautiful in your moving meditation.

Listen to Inspiring People

Listening to an inspiring speaker can raise your spirit.
There are some truly gifted spiritual teachers whose talks
can help you get traction on lifting your spirits. Some of the
best ones have had failures and setbacks, so they know
how you are feeling. They share how they found ways to
raise their spirit and rise up above rock bottom. These
inspiring speakers and authors could become one of your
archetypes. When you are feeling low you can ask yourself
what they might say or do.

Dancing

A couple of quotes for you to get the idea:

> *"you've gotta dance like there's nobody is watching".*[69]

> *"It was the dancing when my little boy Dimitri died...and everybody was crying... Me, I got up and I danced. They said, "Zorba is mad." But it was the dancing — only the dancing that stopped the pain."*[70]

Humans have been dancing since before recorded history.
It is an instinctive, intuitive and original means of raising
the spirit. Don't worry about how it looks, don't do it for

---

[69] William J. Perkley; "you've gotta dance like there's nobody watching, love like you will never be hurt, sing like there is nobody watching."

[70] *Zorba, in Zorba the Greek (full quote)*

reasons of ego, just let go and dance.

Perspective

You can, at will, change your perspective.[71] In the chapter "A Matter of Perspective" you find out that true power includes the ability to see any situation from different perspectives. These perspectives can shape your emotional response and set your mood. The power lies in your ability to choose the appropriate perspective. You can learn to raise your spirit by changing your perspective. Here are some examples:

Gratitude

Use gratitude to change attitude. Sometimes, when you feel down and out about your situation, you can look around and remember what all you do have. As your appreciation rises, so will your spirit. Things could be worse, so the sooner you begin to raise your spirit the better you can endure.

Appreciation

When you are feeling deprived over the loss of something or someone, it can help to appreciate or be thankful for what you still have, and to be thankful you had that someone or something in your life for as long as you did. Appreciation is a good feeling. Good feelings help raise the spirit. Being thankful has a very strong karmic value too.

---

[71] See the chapter "a matter of perspective" in Section One

Communing

Unifying, joining with external positive sources can help raise the spirit. The love you experience being with someone you love, and who loves you is very inspiring. Being at one with the beauty and grandeur of nature can also be inspiring and can help lift your spirit. Here are some examples to try:

Being with other people

Communing with a group of inspired people is truly a blessing. Some of the most powerful ways to raise the spirit are when a group of people gets together to help someone out. You can feel the collective spirit in Habitat Homebuilding, in working in a soup kitchen, in helping out at the food bank, or in taking a toy to needy children at Christmas. When spiritual people get together, the collective spirit is very powerful, and if you are open to it, your spirit will be raised. There is a spiritual synergy that happens when people embrace virtue and join their spirits collectively.

Group Spiritual Practices:

Group Tai Chi

If you have ever performed Tai Chi with a group of people, then hopefully you had the incredible experience of feeling the quickening of the spiritual energy. When it rises and joins with the others, your spirit will rise to an extraordinary measure.

Group Yoga

I once attended a large yoga spiritual event, here in Athens Georgia. I was invited to be one of the mediators holding the space for the event. So even though I do not practice yoga, I was able to join in with the collective spiritual raising, and it was truly awe-inspiring. If you can imagine what it is like for hundreds of people to join in spirit with the single intention of spiritual peace, then you will understand its power.

Group Meditation

More specifically, group meta-meditation can be a powerful means of raising the spirit. Each join with their consciousness into a collective stillness. From this stillness and calm abiding, they send love, peace, and harmony to others. This joining will create the space for you to raise your spirit. The only obstacle would be the ego finding reasons to stay within its self-created prison of gloom.

Communing with Nature

This is a simple concept, communing with nature; yet so powerful. Only the prison of ego can keep you from realizing the relationship between spirit and nature. When you transcend the walls of ego, you will realize that nature is the manifestation of spirit. It is fascinating, glorious, awe-inspiring, and spiritual all at the same time.

Sunsets and Sunrises

Watching the sunrise is one of the simplest forms of meditation that a person can practice. If you have never experienced the rising of spirit as you observed a gorgeous sunrise, then you truly are trapped in an ego prison. You just sit and observe. Try not to think about much, just be at one with it. When our species evolved the Tao gifted us with the potential to appreciate the beauty of color. From within the distraction of your low-spirit, you will miss it. Yet if you get up and go to the window or better yet, go outside and observe, your spirit will drink in the raw beauty of the cosmos.

A sunrise will help raise your spirit at the beginning of the day. A sunset will raise your spirit at the end of the day. In those moments, nothing else matters. Just be one with the experience and let the beauty of it raise your spirit. Know that you are a child of the Tai and that is a spiritual gift.

Plants

I have the good fortune to live near the Georgia Botanical Gardens near Athens, Georgia. It never fails to lift my spirit to go and be with the plants they grow. You can witness every possible color, from species both indigenous and from other parts of the world. This meditation is practiced using the eyes, nose, and sense of touch. The designers have used both exotic and simple plants to create art in various landscape design projects. I feel my spirit rise when I look at the beautiful color of a flower. From the stillness of a tiny seed, the creative power of the Tao creates a natural work of art. My spirit rises when I realize that the Tao also gave me the ability to appreciate it. Being a part of the Tao in this way helps me rise above the pettiness that the ego can trap me in.

Animals

As I write this, it is Spring. The birds are migrating back
north from somewhere south of here. Around our early
flowers and bird feeder are all sorts of interesting and
beautiful birds. When I walk on my favorite trail, in the
woods near me, other animals are going about their lives
with a natural intention. Watching animals, I am reminded
of a passage by the Chinese philosopher Kou Hsiang,

*"All things are what they are, without knowing why
and how they are."*

Leaving the craziness of our species to be at one with the
non-human citizens of the woods helps me to raise my
spirit. These creatures help me transcend the unpleasant
and self-destructive nature of the human ego.

Children

I am very fortunate to be a father and a grandfather. I have
learned a lot from my kids and grandkids. I do not seek
them out for the intended purpose of raising my spirit, it
just happens. Children have an innocence that is priceless.
Not long after they are born, they will open their eyes.
Instinctively they know to make eye contact with you. They
look straight into your soul with an innocence that is
profound. When you can focus your eyes on their eyes
something deeply spiritual will happen. This pure, innocent
little spirit is connecting with your spiritual essence. Let

them "see" you. Let the love pour out of you and into them. Don't hide, don't run, just hold the moment. This rarefied moment will raise your spirit. Don't hide, don't look away, and don't hold back. Just commune with this person. Treat this is a gift, and I hope you can experience it and appreciate its power to awaken and cleanse you.

Helping Others

Having compassion and helping people is a means of raising the spirit by moving beyond your own neediness and embracing benevolence. Giving is its own reward and the reward is spiritual. When you share yourself and help others without expectations your spirit will rise and you will know mystic virtue. When you recognize that you can help someone else, your spirit automatically rises. You are no longer thinking of "me," and that is always a first step in transcending ego and becoming spirit. As you see appreciation and joy in the other, you will experience the same feeling. This is especially powerful when you are in bad shape yourself. Moving beyond your own melancholy to help another in need, simply because you care, will inspire you to continue practicing strategies for raising your own spirit.

Allow Hope

Sometimes the ego will resist hope. It wants to give up. You may have the feeling of "what is the use in hoping, I will just be disappointed all over again." When you are mindful this voice, try to have true courage and allow hope to help you rise out of the dark place you are in. Allowing hope is a kind of self-love that you must allow to flourish. Try a Metta meditation and concentrate on the words. Allow the words to give hope and raise your spirit.

Here is a common metta meditation that Buddhists use. Say each stanza twice then repeat the whole sequence. If you belong to a group, have everyone sing, chant, or say the words aloud. I have found this practice to be soothing and restorative.

May I be filled with love and kindness

May I be well

May I be peaceful and at ease

And may I be happy (2 times)

May you be filled with love and kindness

May you be well

May you be peaceful and at ease

And may you be happy (2 times)

May we be filled with love and kindness

May we be well

May we be peaceful and at ease

And may we be happy. (2 times)

Repeat all.

Raising the spirit is much more than just a survival strategy. It is how you will not only endure; but thrive. Raising the spirit is attaining the Tao. You can empower yourself by learning and practicing meditation, mindfulness, and following the Tao. The is the way of the Sovereign.

42

MODERATE JUDGMENT

"...Respectful response and scornful response
How much is the difference?
Goodness and evil
How much do they differ...?
Chapter 20, Verses 2-4, Tao Te Ching

The Practice: First seek to understand what is really going on before automatically reacting with a value judgment.[72] Cultivate the ability to gain a better perspective by considering virtues such as empathy, patience, and compassion.

This strategy is super simple in theory but difficult in application. It takes practice through experience to cultivate the ability to be patient and resist emotional impulses.

The Application: Be present and use your discerning mind to know the moment. Restrain the impulse to immediately react with a value judgment before considering what is really going on. Seek the facts and truthful meaning. Then

---

[72] Value judgment is a determination or assessment as to whether something or someone is good or bad.

you are better prepared for what to do or say next. In that moment of discernment, postpone value judgment as an option for later determination. To discern is to perceive, recognize, distinguish, and discover the deeper truth without the ego's influence.[73]

Reserving value judgment opens the way to mystic virtue[74] and wu wei[75]. In this way you can avoid painful mistakes that unnecessarily hurt yourself and others.
As you begin to gain sovereignty over the ego you will begin to pay attention to how you react to your daily interactions with others. People will love and trust you if you can be patient and moderate your judgment. You may be able to turn a non-friendship into a friendship by being supportive instead of judgmental.

Misjudging will create problems where there were none. When you leap to the wrong conclusion you might misjudge something that was seen or said. Your actions will then propagate throughout life in a wave of drama karma that can create obstacles and problems in all kinds of ways and with all kinds of people. All beings on our planet are connected one way or the other. Like ripples in a pond, your misjudgment can move outward in waves of destruction.

You may misjudge a situation and miss out on the

---

[73]The authors definition; relevant as a means of finding out what the deeper understanding is of something or someone. They key to this is the distinction between seeking to know and judgment (good and bad).
[74] See Chapter 6, Mystic Virtue.

[75] See Chapter 11, Wu Wei.

opportunity of a lifetime. And what if you had a chance to help someone in a positive meaningful way but misjudged them. And what about our political process where the object is for one politician to cause misjudgment of the other. Voting is an act of judging and one of immense importance. Have you ever realized later that you misjudged the candidate you voted for, or didn't vote for? What if you used discernment before making the decision. This means that you should conduct your own research rather than rely on the judgment of others (media).

Moderate Value Judgment

Since truth is subjective and not absolute you can realize that your truth may not be the same as someone else's.

Cultivating sovereignty includes avoiding absolutes. In chapter 7, A Matter of Perspective, you are advised to avoid fixation on one perspective. Therefore, you should moderate your response and permit value judgment when it is necessary and required. It is a case by case basis. As mentioned before, the best way forward is to be patient and consider things from different perspectives. Let your experience and wisdom guide you.

Karma[76] is another very important reason for moderating judgment and recognizing how judgmental actions work.

---

[76] See Chapter 5, Karma (cause and effect)

Choice, action, and destiny are linked through karma. Karma is a teacher from which you cannot hide.

Value judgment can be sourced in the arrogance of the ego. I have found that when I incorrectly value judge someone the karmic payback is always right around the corner. It is eerily consistent and quick.

One day I was strolling, with my family, along a busy street downtown. I was pushing a stroller with one of my grandkids in it. We were waiting to cross a busy side street when the "walk" sign began flashing. As we stepped off of the curb, a car coming from the side, approaching rapidly as if it wasn't going to stop. When I looked at the driver, I could see that he was a college aged kid texting on his phone. He looked up and slammed on his breaks. He stopped in plenty of time, but it was enough to make me jump in alarm. My alarm quickly became anger. In my self-righteous value judgment, I said some words that my grandchild shouldn't have heard.

We continued walking down the road and my wife asked me if it was going to rain. I whipped out my phone to check out the weather forecast. As we approached the next intersection, everyone else stopped at the curb to wait for the walk light, but I was so distracted looking down at my phone, that I stepped down into the path of an oncoming car. The driver, another college aged kid, honked and veered around me shouting "crazy tourist." There I am standing like a deer in the headlights having had my life pass before my eyes. I suddenly realized that I had done the very thing that I had judged the first college kid for. I only had to travel 2 blocks before karma came back to teach me a lesson. I was lucky. This lesson did not end in tragedy.

If you hate being judged, then learn to not be so quick to judge others. You may notice that people who you do not judge will often give you a break and not be so judgmental of you.

A complement of discernment could be empathy. By trying to understand someone without judging them is to put yourself in their shoes. You can begin to understand how they feel. One you have walked a mile in their shoes, you will realize what they are going through. It is difficult to feel compassion while your mind is filled with negative value judgment.

As always, moderation is the key. There are times when value judgment is appropriate and wise. There are times when you know what someone is saying and doing is wrong. The lesson is to be aware and mindful of your thoughts, actions, and choices.

Discernment and non-judgment are powerful tools of the Tao Sovereign. When the time comes for judgment, act with understanding and truth for that is what you will experience through karma. To reign in the ego and moderate value judgment is sovereignty.

Life Is A Sacred Journey

43

LIFE, A SACRED JOURNEY

Coming into life, entering death
The followers of life, three in ten
The followers of death, three in ten
Those whose lives are moved toward death
Also three in ten
Why? Because they live lives of excess
I've heard of those who are good at cultivating life
Traveling on the road, they do not encounter rhinos or tigers
Entering into an army, they are not harmed by weapons
Rhinos have nowhere to thrust their horns
Tigers have nowhere to clasp their claws
Soldiers have nowhere to lodge their blades
Why? Because they have no place for death
Chapter 50, Tao Te Ching

> Life is Sacred.
> Life is a sacred journey.[77]
> It is a journey of experience.
> It is a spiritual journey.
> Life is experiencing.
> Life is a sacred journey.

We believe ourselves to be the highest order of intelligent life on this planet. However, we are arguably the most distracted species when it comes to being alive and experiencing life. Here in the United States, I have observed our society become seduced into all sorts of mental addictions. A good example would be television programming. Watching TV creates a deep conditioning that can lead to a long-term state of distraction. To sit mesmerized for hours on end with the mind absorbed in non-reality diverts and captivates our focus and attention. We begin to lose the ability to focus our attention at will. The result is that we lose our ability to keep our attention focused and present. We also become confused between the false reality of TV land and real life. This a state of illusion in which we are disconnected from the reality of life. Being apart from reality is to be apart from life. If we do this long enough, it becomes a permanent condition.

When distraction separates you from reality, it disconnects you from your purpose in life. Your purpose in life is to be consciously aware of the living experience. Experiencing life is our continuous journey, step by step, day by day. Through experience and learning we can gain wisdom and

_____

77Some object to the use of the word journey as a metaphor for life experience. Please see my explanation in the notes section at the back of this book.

evolve spiritually. Experiencing life is your sacred duty. Cultivating life does not mean we must abstain from watching television altogether. We are to use moderation to prevent excessive distraction.

A Moment of Truth

Humanity has always had a problem with appreciating the sanctity of life. Through the ages, humans have demonstrated a profound disregard for life. Our history is filled with war. Humans have slaughtered other species to the point of extinction.

Take a moment. Can you remember how precious life is? When someone we love is taken from us, we remember in a primal way just how precious life is. In those moments, we reach for spiritual guidance to help us endure. In these moments of truth, we wake up and realize where we are and what is happening. Sometimes these moments of truth are excruciating, and sometimes they are a moment of bliss such as a first kiss or the birth of a child. Awareness is the conscious experiencing and connection to life. Therefore, life is a precious journey. [78]

Not only is life precious, but it's not as ordinary as the ego would have us believe. Anytime you sense yourself judging something as ordinary, realize that this is the ego's influence on your state of mind. Here is an example. Stop what you are doing and close your eyes. In your mind, look for a memory where you experienced a moment of truth. It may be a moment when you received some big news or a discovery with profound discovery. Possibly it will be a memory from when you received bad news about a health

---

[78] See the word "Journey As A Metaphor for life" in Notes after the glossary.

condition, or the loss of a loved one. If you have ever witnessed the birth of a child time seems to stop; that moment is all that exists. Remember a profound moment where time seemed to slow down, and your life came to a standstill.

When you are in a moment and fully experiencing the flow of reality around you, it is anything but ordinary.

It is the ego, and its insatiable desire that finds life mundane. To experience life, you must rise above distraction and awaken to life as the spiritual being you truly are.

Self-Reflection

As you reflect on your life and you relive a place in your memory you have, with your mind, traveled back to a previous experience. Through consciousness, a bridge has formed between this 'now' and a 'now' in the past. You are in the present and reliving the other simultaneously. Does this meet the criteria for being classified as a quantum event? It really doesn't matter. What does matter is how you remember what it feels like to be connected to life in a spiritual sense. The mind is how we interface with life through perception, so it matters if you can pay attention to how it is affecting your state of being. Transcending the mind is meditation. Intentionally paying attention to it in a non-judgmental way is mindfulness.[79] The ability to be present and in control of the mind and ego is the root of sovereignty. The mind revisits the past frequently, especially in moments of fear. The ego relives moments of

---

[79] To transcend is to rise above, move beyond, leave behind. In this study it is to be free of ego influence.

the past but never appreciates the lesson from the previous experience. The ego worries about what might happen in the future. It creates a prison that traps you between fear and worry. Being mindful of this, the Tao cultivator can use sovereignty over ego and use wisdom to manage the emotional state.

Look at your life. Be honest, and see where you are on your sacred journey. Many have lost their true identity and their true life in the distracted state of ego. We all have life experiences that knock us off the path. With sovereignty (discipline over ego), the true self deals with them and continues with the life experience. If you have lost your way you look for it by waking up. You must wake up and remember how precious life is. When you do, you cultivate the ability to remain awake and present in the full consciousness of life. Your spiritual essence is your true nature. Your true self in charge is sovereignty. Through experience you are able to cultivate wisdom.

Wisdom is gained and cultivated through practice. The opportunity for cultivating wisdom is found each time we experience an obstacle, challenge, or opportunity. When we face a new experience we often have a moment for consideration. In that moment we can put aside any value judgment and view the new experience from various perspectives. We can compare it with previous experiences we had, we can consider the wisdom others might share, and we can listen to our instinct and intuition. Wisdom keeps us on the path.

Your Sacred Duty

If life is a sacred journey, then sovereignty is a sacred duty. You do not have to become an expert. Just implementing some of these insights, in small ways, can change everything in the best possible way. Because life is always changing, there will always be challenges and obstacles. It is how we react to these situations that will affect our wellbeing and destiny. Your sacred duty is to live and learn these lessons through experience. As you transcend distraction and awaken as your true spiritual self, you can realize your true path and follow it. Your true path or your true way of life and being is the sacred journey. Find it, live it. Be the Sovereign.

Life Is A Sacred Journey

About The Author

GLOSSARY OF TERMS

Self

Defined: A being's subjective realization of identity that is separate from others.

In this book, subjectivity is used in two basic ways: the true self and the ego-self.

True Self

- Awakened and Self Aware
- Realization of being spirit-consciousness within the physical world; spirit having a physical experience
- Self-awareness is a state of being that evolves as one realizes that they are more than just a physical form that thinks and reacts.
- The True self is your spiritual identity as a living physical being.

Self-awareness

- A state of consciousness that transcends the ego-identity
- An evolving state of spiritual awareness
- The aspect of self that witnesses the thoughts
- The self-identity that realizes that it is separate from thoughts
- realizes that you are not your thoughts
- Spiritual conscious awareness

- The realization, through meditation, that you are a spiritual being having a physical experience.
- The aspect of self that is aware that it is a spiritual being having a physical experience
- The highest state of awareness
- Awakened from thinking and distraction.
- The spiritual self can control the ego-self.
- The part of you that can control the attention of the mind
- The part of you that can concentrate the attention of the mind for spiritual intention
- At one with the Tao
- Through stillness of the mind (observing without thought), the realization that you are the Tao (source)

Enlightenment

- Fully realized as a spiritual being
- State of being that transcends the ego-self and its suffering
- Is unity with the Tao, Universe, God, Nature
- Is Attainment of the Tao
- Is evolving by degree of transcendence
- Sovereignty over ego
- The end of self-destruction and suffering
- As a transcended consciousness, it observes the activity of the mind in a non-reactive way (mindfulness)

God consciousness

- The spiritual consciousness that is in communion with God (creator)

Buddha Nature

- The luminous mind
- Pure consciousness
- The True Self is the only way to manage and control the ego. This ability is known as sovereignty.
- The true self seeks attainment with the Tao and enlightenment.

Ego-Self

- The physical aspect of self that is highly intelligent but has not evolved spiritually
- The Ego is not aware of its deeper motivations, intentions, personality, reactions. The ego is characterized as a state of being that identifies with how it feels and what it desires.

Examples:
- "I am tired"
- "I am bad"
- "I am a valid person because I am wealthy, a boss, a teacher etc. "
- "I want that"
- "I need that"
- The quality of life is defined by state of consciousness

- Self-worth
- Sanity (how it looks)
- Its possessions

Ego-self is:

- Unhappy unless it always wins
- Unhappy if seen as less beautiful/handsome than another
- Mood is affected by thoughts of how its seen by others
- The interactive part of the mind that is impulsive and reactive to perception about self-esteem
- The ego-self is reactive (as opposed to discernment first and careful consideration of choice)
- Has little ability to exercise patience before reacting.
- The ego-self frequently overreacts to a perceived threat
- The aspect of mind that suffers from stress and emotion
- Uses judgment to define what it perceives (as opposed to discernment)
- Stress response (flight or fight) to what is experienced
- The aspect of mind and personality that is a prisoner to desire.
- Frequently becomes addicted to sensual fulfillment
- Copes with bad feelings and unhappiness with self-destructive activities
- Forms self-destructive habits that become addictions
- Cannot stop itself
- Cannot control its actions

- Will do stupid things even when it knows better
- The part of a person that is subject to distraction.
- The ego-self has unreal expectations of how life should be.
- When the ego-self experiences obstacles or problems it experiences suffering (unhappiness)
- Because the ego is constantly at war with life it seeks to disconnect from it through distraction.
- Seeks to escape life's suffering through distraction
- Distractions become addictions.
- Domination over awareness is on a sliding spectrum depending on life's challenges
- Self-esteem moves up and down a spectrum of unhappiness and self-destruction.
- Seeks distraction and is distracted depending on how problematic life is.
- On good days the ego can remain hidden, and the person may seem spiritual.
- On bad days the ego can cause insane destruction on an imaginable scale.

The ego abhors or fears:
- Virtue
- Discipline
- Altruism
- Helping others first
- Spirituality
- Patience
- Sharing

- Compassion
- Honesty

The ego is the great pretender

- Pretends at spirituality when it can benefit from being seen as spiritual
- Loves complexity and trickery to get ahead in the world
- Pretends to serve others when it senses an advantage
- Constructs self-serving rules to help it get ahead at the expense of others (religious dogma)
- Pretends to care only to get inside another's defenses
- The ego-self denies truth and reality, especially when it is painful, boring, or unfulfilling.
- Avoids dealing with reality when it is too hard, too painful, or interferes with its agendas
- Pretends that things are ok when they are not
- Cannot take ownership of its actions when:
  - it looks bad to others
  - will affect self-esteem
  - interferes with sensual pleasure
  - life does not appear as it should (does not follow some internal agenda)
- The ego-self views enlightenment as a stupid waste of time but will pretend to be enlightened.
- The ego-self will pretend to be spiritual to gain an advantage.

Stillness

- Stillness is pure being.
- The space between thoughts
- Detached observation
- Non-Doing
- Observation (non-thinking)

Detachment

To be aware, non-reactive, observant; unattached action

Silent Witness, The Observer

- The detached, non-reactive observer; the true-self, pure consciousness
- The Observer is the consciousness that observes the activity of the mind. It has a subject-object relationship with thinking. That part of you which realizes that you are not your thoughts.

Detached Observation

To observe independent emotion and the reactive ego

Notes

Journey as A Metaphor for Life

Most people are aware of the word journey as a means of conveyance from one place to another. It is to travel from here to there. However, there is another definition that carries a different perspective. There is also the definition of being in a state of passing or progressing from one stage to another, similar in meaning to evolving. The nature of this meaning is congruent with Tao principles. Accordingly the term journey is a metaphor for the moment by moment experience of passage through life. Life is a matter of experience for evolving spiritually.

Nature (Tao) created the human brain to perceive reality in snippets of cognition. Even this follows the Tao principles of Yin & Yang; advancing and returning. The Tao is a binary system that is always changing from one state to another. Our mind/brain follows this principle by both perception and discernment. This is how we naturally experience the passage or "journey." The premise of this book is to be awake, aware, and consciously observing and interacting in each moment of perception. I submit that the realization of this passage as a conscious effort is a self-evident enlightenment.

Front Cover Photo

The photo on the front cover is an Apple Tree in the wild. It was taken in the Appalachian Mountains near the Georgia-North Carolina border in the Standing Indian State Park.

Excerpts That Others Have Found Meaningful

There were some particular paragraphs that were noted as meaningful by the people who helped to edit and proof this book. We decided to share some of those. My editor called them "pow!"

Dancing to Raise the Spirit

Humans have been dancing since before recorded history. It is an instinctive, intuitive, and original means of raising the spirit. Don't worry about how it looks, don't do it for reasons of ego, just let go and dance. Chapter 41

Communing with Nature (Raising the Spirit)

This is a simple concept, communing with nature, yet so powerful. Only the prison of ego can keep you from realizing the relationship between spirit and nature. When you transcend the walls of ego you will realize that nature is the manifestation of spirit. It is fascinating, glorious, awe-inspiring and spiritual all at the same time. Chapter 41

Sunsets and Sunrises (Raising the Spirit)

Watching the sunrise is one of the simplest forms of meditation that a person can practice. If you have never experienced the rising of spirit as you observed a gorgeous sunrise, then you are truly trapped in an ego prison. You just sit and observe. Try not to think about much, just be at one with it. When our species evolved, the Tao gifted us with the potential to appreciate the beauty of color. From within the distraction of your low-spirit, you will miss it. Yet if you get up and go to the window or better yet, go outside and observe, your spirit will drink in the raw beauty of the cosmos. Chapter 41

Waking Up to Presence (Cultivate Meditation & Mindfulness)

I had become conditioned to wake up every hour. This practice began to make a big difference in my behavior and stress level. At least once an hour, I could wake up and realize what I was doing and make smarter choices. Often that choice was one to relax and distress. Soon I was even able to wake up and think about what I had been doing and if it was in line with my personal goals.

Then I set my watch to beep every thirty minutes. Moreover, like before, I soon became conditioned to wake just before the alarm beeped and become present. My performance as a boss and leader improved dramatically. In every one of those awake moments, I could choose to listen and pick a wise and virtuous response. I learned to be empathetic, inspired, cheerful, insightful, and understanding. Our team began to perform better, and things ran a lot smoother. I began to enjoy my job. There were still problems and obstacles, but my new-found powers allowed me to work through them effectively. I also learned to create fewer problems by making smarter choices. Chapter 28

Distraction

Distraction is the state of not being present. It is a part of life, but it must be managed and moderated. It becomes a problem when we get so caught up in the drama of the moment that we are unaware that we have slipped back over into the ego-self. Have you ever looked back on a really stupid thing you did and realized that you knew better but just lost control? Have you ever said something in a moment of passion that you deeply regret? When you look back on it, you will realize that you were just angry or frustrated. Even though it is understandable, it is not right.

Imagine being able to see what you are about to do or say

and then step back from it and choose to do or say something else. Even though you are experiencing this storm of emotions, you do not have to give in to them. That is the power of the transcended self. Chapter 28

The Critical Moment of Choice

I have had many conversations with people about how to cultivate self-discipline. Self-discipline is exercised in a moment of choice. Lack of self-discipline is the ego always following the desire of the moment. Alternatively, sometimes a loss of discipline happens when raw emotion overwhelms us. Fear and anger can drive us to take self-destructive actions. In the critical moment of choice, you will be faced with whether you will give in to it or not. Chapter 27

The Silent Witness

If you practice enough, there will come a time when your skill matures into a relaxed transition into the stillness. You will know when this happens because you will be free from the pull of ego and mind-wandering. You become the silent witness. This is becoming consciously aware without actively thinking about it. This is the center of being. The more you can experience this state, the more you become a part of this nature. Chapter 27

Mindfulness

Mindfulness is being able to pay attention to mind and mood in a state of detached observation. With mindfulness, you will see the ego-self rising but not let it do the choosing. So even though you may have all sorts of desires and passions, you will choose the right way. That is self-discipline. Chapter 27

Wisdom is rooted in the True-Self

You can come up with a whole list of wise life strategies,

but if you cannot break the control of ego, you will fail. It is the reason smart people some very stupid things. Wise strategies must be rooted in the true self. This is your spiritual identity as a living being, so it through this state of being that you cultivate your life strategies and live by them with discipline. Chapter 27

Want versus Need

The question to ask is "why did I want this." If you can be honest with yourself, you can see how you waste many resources in pursuit of that which cannot be found. Chapter 27

Listening

"You can hear a lot just by listening"

Chapter 36

Lying to Yourself

The one thing that is worse than lying to others is lying to yourself. Dishonesty to your true self is a form of non-acceptance. The source of self-deception is, of course, the ego. Acceptance of reality as it is is a function of sovereignty. Sovereignty is true power. Chapter 34

Truth as A Weapon

The cunning and clever ego will sometimes use words of truth with the intention of defeating or hurting another. While it is important to be truthful with others the intention behind using truth is what matters. The ego by nature is not caring nor compassionate so it will use words of truth as a damaging weapon. Truth can be very hurtful and can even destroy someone's wellbeing. Truth should never be used to hurt someone or to get ahead of them. Chapter 37

Use Wisdom to Create Your Destiny

Glossary

I define wisdom as the intelligence that consciously combines knowledge and experience for sound judgment. Many books and articles use the phrase "Wisdom of the Tao." I take that to mean, intelligence gained through study and practice of Tao lessons in everyday life. However, it is important to note the distinction between knowing the wisdom and using the wisdom. Acquiring knowledge alone is not enough. To benefit from the real power of wisdom, you must cultivate it and use in the moment to moment choosing that creates your destiny. Chapter 20

Don't Let the Ego Override Your Wisdom

The other point to know is that the gained experience must be applied. Wisdom has no value if you do not listen to it and use it. This may sound mundane, but it happens every time your ego overrides your wisdom. It is the reason that smart people make stupid mistakes. Chapter 20

Choose Softness

It takes self-discipline of ego control to choose softness. Self-control and ego management is the greater principle of sovereignty. In the moment of action, you have a choice. If you are mindful of ego, you can be detached from reacting. Chapter 23

Accumulate Virtue

Accumulating virtue means there is nothing one cannot overcome

When there is nothing that one cannot overcome

One's limits are unknown

Chapter 59, Verses 5 -7, Tao Te Ching (Chapter 1)

Cultivate Sovereignty as If Your Life Depended On it

Some key words to note here are "*everlasting, longevity and lasting vision.*" Sovereignty is the *mother principle of power* which gives you endurance to experience a long physical life and evolve spiritually (enlightenment.) Sovereignty is the constancy of spirit. Sovereignty is being. Sovereignty is the Tao (the way) of longevity and lasting vision. Therefore, you should cultivate Sovereignty as if your life depended on it because guess what, it does. Sovereignty is being the ruler over the emotional, desire seeking ego so that you can attain the Tao. Chapter 1

How to Take Charge of Your Destiny

Why is this so important? Mindfulness and meditation are necessary to take charge of your destiny. Destiny is the result of choices you make each moment of each day. Sovereignty is the ability to take charge of your destiny and rule over the ego along with its influences over the mind and emotions. Therefore, to transform your life into one of joy and success you must cultivate the ability to practice mindfulness and be the Sovereign. Chapter 4

About Karma

"If you want to know your past,

look at your present conditions.

If you want to know your future,

look at your actions today."

Chinese Proverb- Unknown

Chapter 5

To Experience Life You Must Rise Above Distraction

When you are in a moment and fully experiencing the flow of reality around you, it is anything but ordinary. It is only the ego, and its insatiable desire that finds life mundane. To experience life you must rise above distraction and awaken to life as the spiritual being you truly are. Chapter 42

Cultivate Wisdom

You must cultivate wisdom through practice. The opportunity for cultivating wisdom is found in each time we experience an obstacle, challenge or opportunity. When we face a new experience we often have the moment for consideration. At that moment, you can put aside the judgment and view the new experience from various perspectives. We can compare it with previous experiences we have had. We can consider what wisdom others might share. We can listen to our instinct and intuition.

Wisdom keeps you on the path to continue the journey of life. Chapter 42

Meditation

Meditation is a state of being, and a higher state of consciousness. Being able to bring your focused attention above and beyond the crazy mindstream of thought and emotion is the most powerful skill that you can attain. It is also the hardest skill that you will ever work on cultivating. It takes practice. In the beginning, meditation practice is the most difficult. It can also be very difficult during times of striving and suffering. Ironically the times we need stillness the most is when the ego will reject it the hardest. If you are new to meditation, you must remember that you have been conditioned all of your life for undisciplined mind-wandering. Focus and concentration are skills that you cultivate through practice. Chapter 4

Be mindful of emotions

Only if you are mindful of your emotions, feelings, choices, and actions can you wisely navigate life to accomplish long-term goals. Goal achievement lies somewhere in the future. The steps you take to reach that point in your destiny are made right here and right now. That moment of choice is the point whether you remain true to yourself or fail at self-discipline. You must have virtuous clarity in picking your strategies and goals otherwise you will be serving the ego's path of desire. Chapter 4

Allowing the ego to control decision making

When the ego has too much control over decision making and choices trouble and suffering ensue. The ego abhors wisdom and will default to whatever desire happens to be prevailing. It will ignore the wise choice and tries to fulfill its lust. Ignoring wisdom and following ignorance will recklessly cause trouble for itself and others. Wise choices create harmony. Chapter 17

Glossary

Judgment and Karma

Karma[80] is another very important reason for moderating judgment and recognizing how judgmental actions work. Choice, action, and destiny are linked through karma. Karma is a teacher from which you cannot hide. Value judgment can be sourced in the arrogance of the ego. I have found that when I incorrectly value judge someone, the karmic payback is always right around the corner. It is eerily consistent and quick. Chapter 42

Life is not mundane

It is the ego, and its insatiable desire that finds life mundane. To experience life, you must rise above distraction and awaken to life as the spiritual being you truly are. Chapter 43

Gaining Wisdom

Wisdom is gained and cultivated through practice. The opportunity for cultivating wisdom is found each time we experience an obstacle, challenge or opportunity. When we face a new experience we often have a moment for consideration. In that moment we can put aside any value judgment and view the new experience from various perspectives. We can compare it with previous experiences we had, we can consider the wisdom others might share, and we can listen to our instinct and intuition. Wisdom keeps us on the path. Chapter 8

---

[80] See Chapter 5, Karma (cause and effect)

Glossary

ABOUT THE AUTHOR

Samuel (Sam) Beasley is regular guy living in North Georgia. He wants to be remembered as just a fellow traveler on the way.

He enjoys Tai Chi, Meditation and Tao discussion. For more about this book and various programs please visit thedixietaoist.com

For book discussion on Facebook: https://www.facebook.com/groups/215926979193783/